CLASSIC ROCK CLIMBS
IN THE
Lake District

BY BILL BIRKETT

The Oxford Illustrated Press

© 1989, Bill Birkett

ISBN 0 946609 56 X

Published by:
The Oxford Illustrated Press Limited, Haynes Publishing Group, Sparkford, Nr Yeovil, Somerset BA22 7JJ, England.

Haynes Publications Inc., 861 Lawrence Drive, Newbury Park, California 91320, USA.

Printed in England by:
J. H. Haynes & Co. Limited, Sparkford, Nr Yeovil, Somerset.

British Library Cataloguing in Publication Data
Birkett, Bill
    Classic rock climbs of the Lake District
    1. Cumbria. Lake District. Rock climbing.
    Manuals
    I. Title
    796.5′223′094278

    ISBN 0-946609-56-4

Library of Congress Catalog Card Number
88-83484

Contents

ACKNOWLEDGEMENTS

Many people helped and encouraged me in the preparation of this book. I would particularly like to thank the following:

Martin Bagness, Dave Belgove, Jim Birkett, Chris Bonington, Gerald Bonington, Greg Cornforth, Ruth Densley, Louise Dickie, Colin Downer, Ralph Fawcett, Mark Glaister, Rick Graham, Mark Greenbank, Tony Greenbank, John Hargreaves, Trevor Jones, Julia Laverock, Jude Lenartowicz, Steve Lenartowicz, Gunárs Libeks, Geneuève Lubas, John Lockley, Al Phizacklea, Susan Lund, Jim Morgan (Guide), Jon Rigby, Merril Sheen, Fred Snallam, Stephanie Snowball, Luke Steer, Sean Tomlinson, John White, Bob Wightman, Brenda Wilkinson.

For correcting the manuscript I would like to thank Susan Lund.

For the use of published material I am indebted to the Fell and Rock Climbing Club, Yorkshire Ramblers Club, the estate of May Wedderburn Cannan, Methuen & Co. Ltd., Heinemann Educational Books Ltd.

Thanks are due to Martin Bagness for the artwork.

Thanks are due to Paul Renouf of Photo-Scope for black and white printing.

DEDICATION

To Jim Birkett and the memory of Bill Peascod—both great free climbing spirits who inspired me profoundly in different ways.

INTRODUCTION

Following *Classic Rock Climbs In Great Britain* this is the first in a series of individual books to cover the five main climbing areas of Britain. The philosophy behind the series is that of portraying the character of the area and the spirit of some of its most outstanding rock climbs. Whatever the degree of difficulty of the routes chosen, their pedigree or antiquity, they have been selected to display a quality best described as classic.

The Lake District naturally falls into six distinct climbing areas with crags that are situated on or are reached from: The Coniston Fells, Wasdale, Great Langdale, The Eastern Fells, Borrowdale and Buttermere. From these areas 51 climbs have been selected and the format of the book is such that there is a fact sheet for each route followed by a summary and description with an accompanying photographic essay of the climb.

Whilst we all climb principally for the fun of it the sport of rock climbing is multifaceted with many different attractions. There is the pure thrill of rock climbing; strong fingers, good balance and mental control conquering naked rock on those days when the climbing hunger seems insatiable, and nothing at all seems impossible. On days like these hard routes such as Lost Horizons or Fear and Fascination may be on your list. There is the wonder of the mountains; the morning dew; sweetness after storm; the sun on your back; the shriek of the peregrine and the howl of the wind; an immense spectrum of experience heightened by your perilous involvement with living rock. Contrasting sensations of a pleasant summer's evening high on the clean North-West Face of Gimmer Crag or on the lonelier walls of Birkness Combe, on the heights of Scafell, Gable and Pillar Rock or the roadside crags of Shepherds or White Ghyll. The joy of good companionship and conversation; the sharing of appreciation, knowledge, laughter and the reliving of the climbing adventure when the day is long done. A comparison of how each fared on the step across the Rochers Perches pitch on Eliminate 'A' or a memory of the crux moves on The Crack perhaps. So many sensations, so many routes, but whatever your particular desire it is intended that the classic climbs detailed here will enhance your climbing enjoyment and liberate the free climbing spirit.

The areas are quite distinct in character and history and whilst modern transport means that most will be able to sample the particular delights of each, their independence and diversity will be found to be one of the most striking attractions of Lake District climbing. In addition to an overall map of the Lake District each area has been sketched to give a three-dimensional representation clearly showing the juxtaposition of the crags as they lie on the fells. As if one was viewing the areas from a strategically flown helicopter it is now easy to see at a glance the whole environment of the climbs and their relative distances from the valley centres and car parks.

A fact sheet and route summary provide all you need to locate and follow the line of the route. The summary follows the conventional system of guidebook route description and is taken from first hand experience. With the advent of modern equipment and rope techniques (see *Modern Rock and Ice Climbing* by the author) it is usual to run out long rope lengths (I recommend 50-m length ropes although in most cases 45m would be adequate) and consequently I have described the pitch lengths to accommodate this now usual style of climbing.

The description of the climb constitutes an essay relating not only the facts, the physical moves, possible protection placements, the history, my own adventures, but strives to capture the unique feeling and spirit of the individual route. I have simply written from the heart and my own enjoyment of the climb. However, I have restrained myself from describing everything about any particular climb, my intention being to whet the appetite only. The full experience—and many surprises—will only be enjoyed by climbing the routes themselves.

The photographic appreciation of the climbs in colour and black and white is intended to display the particular character of the route and the environment in which it is placed. An overlaid black and white photograph also exactly depicts the actual line of each climb providing a rapid but accurate reference to its location and direction.

Achieving high technical standards, being there at the right time at the right split second, is not an automatic procedure in mountain rock climbing photography and there have been times when the casual observer may have felt that the photographer was more precariously placed than the subject itself. Whilst, most certainly, the plates are intended to accurately record the pure physical involvement, climber to rock, I have also designed them to speak of the excitement, joy, solace, drama, peace and beauty of the lonely wild places and of my great love for climbing.

Route Selection and Difficulty

Although I have climbed all the routes in this book, and a few more besides, it may be thought that I mainly climb in the hard route bracket. This impression would not be wholly correct and I have, since commencing the sport under the guidance of my father, Jim Birkett, appreciated the whole spectrum of climbing experience. For a while now, possibly due to the rather artificial influence of climbing magazines, there has been a tendency for polarisation with certain groups of climbers missing out on the complete climbing experience. I think my attitude was summed up by Joe Brown, one of the greatest rock climbers, when he said in an interview with Jim Curran:

'I think the important thing about climbing is not what standard you climb at, but what you get out of it. I just get so much out of it and, I don't know whether, because my memory is never crystal sharp on some things, it's getting older that makes me really appreciate climbing without taking into account its standard. I have been doing classic climbs for a long time . . .'

A book such as this must be finite and there are a number of outstanding climbs that just could not be included—I apologise. Of course *Classic Rock Climbs in Great Britain* selected fifteen routes from the Lake District and this explains their absence here.

Area Notes

The six different areas warrant a separate introduction and first time visitors to the area may find some interest in the following notes.

Area 1—The Coniston Fells Dow is one of the finest climbing cliffs in the Lake District and in midsummer most will supplement the climbing with a dip in Goat's Water. However beware, for this is a high mountain crag and can be extremely bleak when the sun dis-appears and the wind blows. Wallowbarrow offers a complete contrast and is a delightful place to climb at most times of the year. The Sun Inn at Coniston and the Newfield Inn at Seathwaite (observe the uniquely banded slate floor) are the hostelries most frequented by climbers in this area.

Area 2—Wasdale As H. M. Kelly, of Moss Ghyll Grooves (and much else) fame said: '. . . I began to think that there was no place like Wasdale Head. I lost my heart to it so that when Morley Wood tried to inveigle me back to Wales by talking about "a mighty un-climbed cliff" called Clogwyn du'r Arddu, I am afraid that I turned a deaf ear to his entreaties!' The cliffs of Great Gable and Scafell form an impressive horseshoe above the narrow valley of Wasdale and it remains one of the most exciting and rewarding climbing centres in the Lake District. A word of caution, however: should wet weather prevail there are few diversions. The Wasdale Head Inn is the climbers' pub but The Strands and The Screes in Nether Wasdale (and campsite) provide a good alternative.

Area 3—Great Langdale Good clean rock, a large variety of routes and satisfactory wet weather alternatives make this one of the most popular and enjoyable climbing centres. The Old Dungeon Ghyll and the Golden Rule (the latter in Ambleside with climbing land-lord and bunkhouse) are the climbers' pubs.

Area 4—Eastern Fells This is a large area and the two crags selected are chosen for their contrasting qualities. Castle Rock is extremely accessible and user friendly. Dove Crag is remote and very impressive. The best centre is probably Ambleside and there is always the Climbing Wall here should the weather prevent real climbing.

Area 5—Borrowdale Certainly the best wet weather alternatives and most accessible climbs are here and this is probably the most popular of all the valleys. Little wonder because it is arguably the most aesthetically beautiful of all the Lakeland climbing areas. Despite the vegetated appearance of the crags the climbing, at all grades of difficulty, is quite superb. Bentley Beetham, Paul Ross and Pete Livesey are all big names involved with the history of Borrowdale climbing. The Scafell at Rosthwaite (near the head of the valley) and the Packhorse in Keswick are possibly the most frequented pubs here.

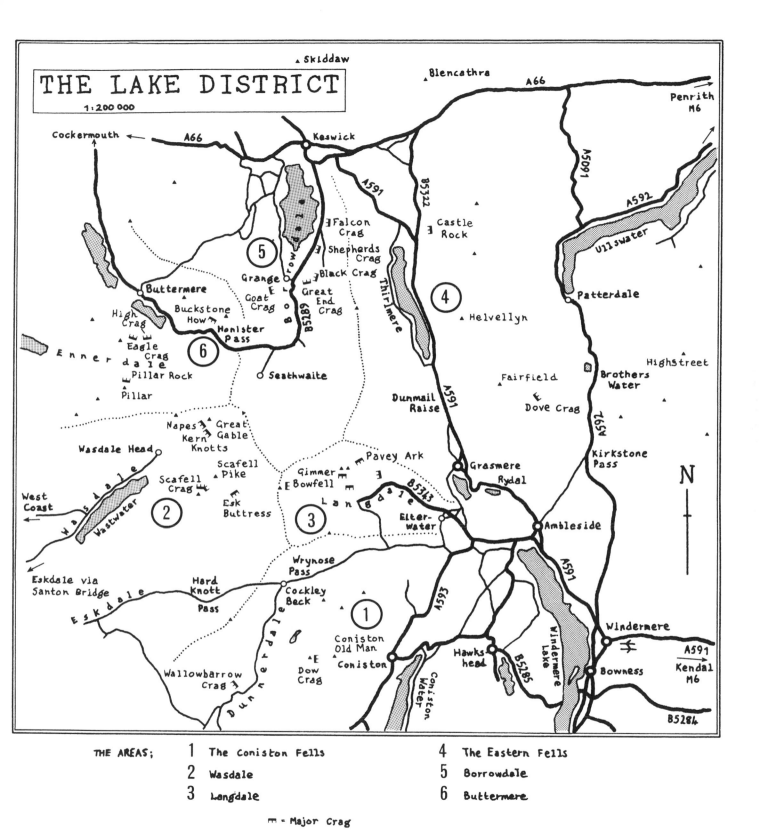

THE LAKE DISTRICT

1:200 000

Skiddaw

Blencathra

A66

Penrith
M6

Cockermouth

A66

Keswick

A591

B5322

A5091

A592

Ullswater

Falcon
Crag

Castle
Rock

Shepherds
Crag

⑤

Grange

Black Crag

Great
End
Crag

Goat
Crag

Thirlmere

④

Helvellyn

Patterdale

Buttermere

Buckstone
How

Borrowdale

B5289

⑥

Honister
Pass

Highstreet

High
Crag

Eagle
Crag

Seathwaite

Dunmail
Raise

Fairfield

Dove Crag

Brothers
Water

Ennerdale

Pillar Rock

A591

Pillar

Napes Great
Gable

Kern
Knotts

Pavey Ark

Kirkstone
Pass

Wasdale Head

Scafell
Pike

Gimmer

Bowfell

B5343

Grasmere

Rydal

West
Coast

Scafell
Crag

Langdale

Wastwater

②

Esk
Buttress

③

Elter-
water

Ambleside

N

Wasdale

Wrynose
Pass

Eskdale via
Santon Bridge

Hard
Knott
Pass

Cockley
Beck

Dunnerdale

①

A593

A591

Windermere
Lake

Windermere

A591
Kendal
M6

Eskdale

Coniston
Old Man

Hawks
head

B5285

Bowness

Wallowbarrow
Crag

Dow
Crag

Coniston

Coniston
Water

B5284

THE AREAS;

1	The Coniston Fells	4	The Eastern Fells
2	Wasdale	5	Borrowdale
3	Langdale	6	Buttermere

⊓ = Major Crag

Area 6—Buttermere Stuck at the northernmost position of all the Lakeland climbing regions Buttermere is the quietest climbing area—and better for it. Bill Peascod is the name I most associate with the climbing here and he dubbed it the 'Cinderella' of Lakeland valleys. Quiet beauty and fine climbs abound here together with the starting point for the most elegant walk to Pillar Rock—the most hallowed of all Lakeland crags. The Fish is possibly the most traditional of the hostelries.

Using This Book

Generally speaking within the selected areas the crags have been selected in a clockwise manner around a particular valley centre and the climbs on these crags have been described starting from the left and working to the right. There are, of course, some exceptions to the rule; notably on the East Buttress of Scafell when the logical approach is in from Mickledore on the right end of the crag—here the climbs are described from right to left. But in all cases the position of the route is clearly described and illustrated.

For each climb there is an introductory list of information which is mainly self-explanatory but the following comments should be noted.

Grading of Climbs: The dual subjective and numerical/alphabetical British system of grading rock climbs has been adopted. The grades apportioned are my own and may be at slight variance with information elsewhere, but should prove consistent throughout the different areas.

Generally within the text only climbs of Very Severe stature and above have been given a technical grading, e.g. Eliminate 'A' – 360ft (110m), Very Severe (Overall Grade) (4c) (Technical Grade of the hardest pitch).

Attitude and Altitude: This information is simple but extremely important to get the best out of the Lakeland weather. By giving sensible thought to the height of the climb above sea level and the direction in which the climb faces, combined with the seasonal climatical divisions in Britain, routes may be selected that can be climbed at some time throughout all twelve months of the year.

For example although the high crags of Scafell may be out of condition from November until May the lower crags in Langdale and Borrowdale may offer worthwhile climbing. It is however not unusual for sun-facing crags, like Esk Buttress and The Napes, despite their altitude to be suitable for climbing at some period during each month of the year, depending on the prevailing conditions and wise selection.

Obviously a south-facing climb will get the sunshine throughout the year: one facing east will get it in the morning; one facing west in the evening and one facing north may never see it at all (depending on the time of the year) or receive its warmth.

The higher the cliff above sea level the colder the air temperature.

Below is a table showing the Overall Grade, which is an impression grade based on the length and seriousness (difficulty in placing protection) and the range of technical difficulty that may be reasonably expected in this overall grade.

Used Together		
British Overall Grade		British Technical Grade
Moderate		1a
Difficult		2a
Very Difficult		2b
Severe (Mild)		2c, 3a
Severe		3a, 3b
Severe (Hard)		3b, 3c
Very Severe (Mild)		4a, 4b
Very Severe		4b, 4c
Very Severe (Hard)		4c, 5a
Extremely Severe	E1	5a, 5b
	E2	5b, 5c
	E3	5c, 6a
	E4	6a, 6b
	E5	6a, 6b
	E6	6b, 6c
	E7	6c, 7a

British Overall Grade and Corresponding Technical (Pitch) Grading.

Descriptions and Descents: All information (unless stated to the contrary) is given looking at the climb (or crag). Therefore *right* and *left* are relative to the climber *facing in*. This is true for both the climbing descriptions and the descents—because it is usual to work out your descent route from the ground, prior to climbing.

Beware also of rock falls, etc., that may subsequently change the character of the route from that described here.

Dangers: Despite modern protection, or what anyone may say to the contrary, rock climbing is potentially dangerous. Anything less than total concentration, and awareness of the dangers, throughout the climbing day can lead to tragedy.

The following is a table comparing the British system of technical grading with some of the most popular grading systems used elsewhere in the world. The table utilises my experiences and those of many others. However, this is not an absolute guarantee of accuracy and is intended as a guide only.

Britain	France	UIAA	USA	Australia
4a	4+V	V	5,6	15
4b	5	V+	5,7	16
4c	5	VI	5,8	17
5a	5+	VI	5,9	18
5b	6a	VI+	5,10a	19
		VII	5,10b	20
5c	6b	VII	5,10c	21
			5,10d	
6a	6c	VII+	5,11a	22
		VIII	5,11b	23
6b	7a	VIII	5,11c	24
		VIII⅃	5,11d	25
6c	7b	IX	5,12a	26
				27
		IX	5,12b	28
7a	7c		5,12c	
		IX+	5,12d	
	8a	X	5,13a	

Table Comparing International Grading Systems.

This book assumes a thorough understanding of, and sound practical ability with, all techniques and equipment currently in use in British rock climbing. Beware of rapidly changing weather, particularly in the mountains. A high, long mountain route is always a serious proposition irrespective of technical difficulty. Always carry adequate clothing, a warm summer's day can rapidly deteriorate.

Photography: All the photography is my own. It is 35mm and is reproduced from colour transparencies and black and white negatives. A variety of lenses have been employed from wide-angle 28mm to a long focal length of 150mm. Further essential information on hill and climbing photography is extensively detailed in the *Hill Walkers Manual* by the author and published by Oxford Illustrated Press.

Good climbing—see you on the crags.

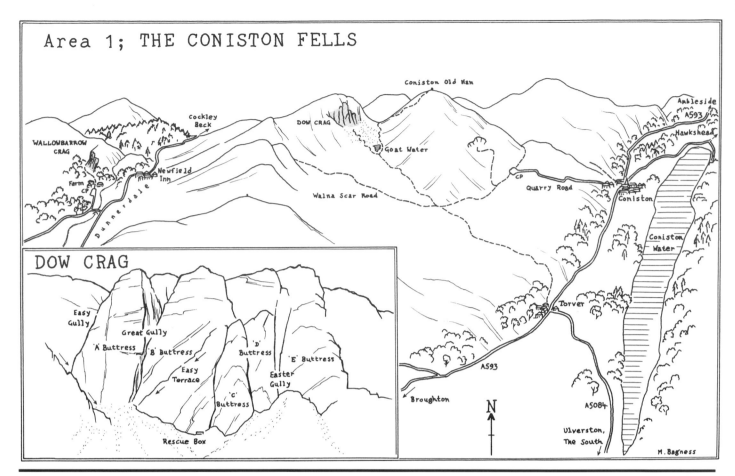

Area 1; THE CONISTON FELLS

DOW CRAG

THE CONISTON FELLS—DOW CRAG

DOW CRAG: Isengard/Samba Pa Ti, Eliminate A, Giant's Crawl, Ordinary Route 'C'.
Map Ref: SD 263978.
Guidebooks: *Rock Climbing in the Lake District* by Birkett, Cram, Eilbeck and Roper. *Scafell, Dow, & Eskdale* (FRCC Guide) by Al Phizacklea.
Attitude: Faces east.
Altitude: 2,000ft (610m).
Rock: Quartz—splashed rhyolite—rough in places with good flake and finger holds.
Access: Take the steep road up from Coniston to the Old Man. Beyond the gate follow the unmetalled road until the Walna Scar track breaks off to the left (Parking here or a few hundred yards further on.) Pass through two rock cuts until a path leads steeply up a grass bank to the right. Continue up and along to Goat's Water. Pass below the tarn and ascend to the crag above. 'A' Buttress lies at the highest point to the left and is separated from 'B' Buttress by the large rift of Great Gully. The best approach from below is to go slightly rightwards aiming for the blue rescue box near the lowest point of the crag (1 hour).
Descent: From the top the best descent for all the routes, except of Ordinary Route 'C', is to the

left (south). Pass Great Gully and avoid the next gully (Easy Gully) because it contains much loose rock. Keep left to find an easy scree rake which brings you down quickly and safely to the foot of 'A' Buttress. For Ordinary Route 'C' the climb finishes some way below the top of the crag, on Easy Terrace. It is best to traverse along this until it steepens where a scrambling descent can be made to emerge not far below the foot of Great Gully, beneath the upper section of 'B' Buttress. Care must be taken not to dislodge any stones as the whole of 'B' Buttress and the point of arrival at the crag all lie directly below.
Observations: Dow is a large crag, one of the finest in the Lake District, and consists of five distinct buttresses. From left to right they are labelled alphabetically starting with 'A' and ending with 'E'. Isengard/Samba Pa Ti and Eliminate 'A' are situated on 'A' Buttress, Giant's Crawl on 'B', Ordinary 'C' on 'C'. There is a large variety of climbing to be found with good routes of all grades. Note the altitude and the attitude can make this an extremely cold crag on which to climb when the sun leaves it in the afternoon.

Facing page, top left:
Rick Graham on Isengard/Samba Pa Ti beginning the roof above the cave stance.

Facing page, top right:
Julie Laverock on the exposed traverse out of the cave on Eliminate 'A'.

Facing page, bottom:
Dow Crag showing routes Giant's Crawl, Ordinary Route 'C'.

10

DOW CRAG

Descent

A
BUTTRESS

EASY TERRACE

EASY GULLY

GREAT GULLY

GIANT'S CRAWL

B
BUTTRESS

C

D

E

RESCUE BOX

ORDINARY ROUTE 'C'

○ belay point

DOW CRAG: Isengard/Samba Pa Ti and Eliminate 'A'

ISENGARD/SAMBA PA TI: 350ft (107m), E2 (5b).
First Ascent: L. Brown, R. McHardy, April 1962/ A Hyslop, R. Graham, 20 August 1977.
ELIMINATE 'A': 360ft (110m), Very Severe (4c).
First Ascent: H. S. Gross, G. Basterfield, 17 June 1923.
Location: 'A' Buttress, Dow Crag, Coniston.
Descent: In addition to that already detailed (see DOW CRAG) a quicker alternative is to descend Abraham's Route which is moderate in difficulty. This is a chimney leading down the left side of the buttress into the lower reaches of Easy Gully and can be located some way below the summit.

Isengard/Samba Pa Ti—Summary

A very direct line up the buttress taking a vague crackline to gain the cave of Eliminate 'A'. From here it pulls boldly through the roof. Start 15ft (4.5m) left of Eliminate 'A' below a short corner crack.

1. 30ft (9m), (4b). The corner leads to a ledge.

2. 130ft (40m), (5b). Bear left up the steepening slab until technical moves through a bulge lead to a long horizontal ledge. Step right to enter a bulging crack. Climb it to the overhang and pull through this at its weakest point to gain a slab leading into the cave.

3. 100ft (30m), (5b). Move up the right edge of the slab to the overhang. Pull straight over, sling on flake held in place with nuts below. Continue up the impending groove, trending rightwards, to the next bulge. Pass it on the right, then move across the steep wall leftwards to belay on the ledge below the obvious crack. (junction with Gordon and Craig's).

4. 90ft (27m), (4b). Follow a line, as directly as possible, 10ft(3m) right of this crack.

Eliminate 'A'—Summary

Start by scrambling to a ledge and belay some 30ft (10m) above the bottom of Great Gully.

1. 45ft (14m), (4b). Traverse right to the edge of the wall overlooking the gully. Move up and slightly right into a groove. Belay on the ledge below a shallow scoop in the middle of the wall above.

2. 75ft (23m), (4b). There is a weakness in the wall that develops into a more definite groove after about 30ft (10m). Take this scoop moving right to make a mantleshelf move to gain the foot of the groove. Climb the groove until it is possible to make an exposed step right and to move up around the corner to large blocks. Gain the top of the blocks and belay.

3. 50ft (15m), (4c). Step boldly and delicately leftwards from the blocks into a precarious corner and gain a standing position on the small ledge. Balance around the rib on the left, stepping down slightly and easily up into the cave to reach a multitude of belays —the Rochers Perches pitch.

4. 55ft (17m), (4b). Take the diagonal ramp leading out leftwards beneath the roof until a pull over an exposed bulge leads to a ledge.

5. 50ft (15m), (4c). Traverse right across the tremendously exposed wall and up to a groove which is followed to a ledge.

Louise Dickie on Isengard, Samba Pa Ti pulling through the overlap into the layback below the cave stance.

DOW CRAG 'A' BUTTRESS

ABRAHAM'S ROUTE

Rochers Perches

ISENGARD/ SAMBA PA TI

ELIMINATE 'A'

EASY GULLY

GREAT GULLY

belay point

Dow Crag showing routes Eliminate 'A', Isengard/Samba Pa Ti, on 'A' Buttress.

Isengard/Samba Pa Ti and Eliminate 'A'—Description

The most striking single buttress on Dow is undoubtedly 'A', offering almost 300ft (90m) of clean unbroken rock. Consisting of three definite sections it rises smooth and vertical at first until after 100ft (30m) it bulges and overhangs. Above this band of overhangs it finally consolidates into a rocky wall. If each part of this elegant rock were separated and stood alone it would still be impressive. The deep cuts of Great Gully to the right and Easy Gully to the left give the buttress its independence, leaving a formidable, inescapable challenge. Eliminate 'A' provides the solution, giving one of the best climbs in the very severe category in this country.

It is a long and remarkably sustained climb taking an impressive line; one which, despite its antiquity, remains modern in both concept and impact. Eliminate 'A' does not compromise, there is no deviation from the challenge; the technicality of the climbing and the exposure are always first class. The line taken up to the large roof and the cave is exacting, there are no possible escapes, and the exposure is with you from when you first commence the rib above Great Gully. Perhaps the hardest section, the technical crux, the Rochers Perches pitch, is actually reaching the cave. But from here the intimidating nature of the large roof above your head, combined with the necessary space-walking along the bottomless ramp leading you away from security and into ground that looks totally hostile, ridicules the purely technical aspects of difficulty. Then if you think that pitch was exposed the traverse across the bottomless wall, above 200ft (60m) of space, is doubly so. This again demands not only a cool-headed lead but neat climbing skill.

The route was climbed as early as 1923 and was a marvellous effort by any standards. Gross was the leader concerned. Like an exploding supernova he appeared without warning, shone with unbelievable brilliance then disappeared from the scene. Within a period of twelve months he pioneered four routes that must always be regarded as among the strongest *tours de force* in Lakeland history. His friend and climbing partner, the man who so effectively introduced him to the sport, 'inviting him to leave the city street and climb', George Basterfield (the Mayor of nearby Barrow), summed it up as follows:

'Apart from the "mixed grill" of climbs embracing every category, there are, on the front-line-

6. 85ft (26m), (4b). The scoop left of the obvious crack is taken (the obvious crack belongs to Gordon and Craig's Route), to a flake beneath an overhang. Attempt to continue as straight as possible over this and up to the top, although numerous ways are possible now.

classic-crag-of-Doe, four supersevere "courses", that admit only the leadership of the highest skilled craftsman. *Doe Crag Traverse, Eliminate A, B and C* are all the creation of the late Herbert Spencer Gross. The sustained severity and thrilling exposure of the rock to be experienced throughout the four courses bears the indelible hallmark of a master craftsman. I could a tale unfold of a prowess bristling with adventure, but enough in the above to have known H. S. G. for a cragsman of the highest order.'[1]

Dow, known as Doe until the 1930s (as it still is by many), was very much the province of the Barrow climbers and from the earliest days until modern times they have had the greatest influence on its history. Of the imposing 'A' Buttress George Bower wrote in his wonderfully descriptive 1922 guidebook (the FRCC 'red' guide):

'The great wall of "A" Buttress, overlooking Great Gully, is as yet unclimbed, and appears likely so to remain until the advent of the future race of climbers, fitted with suctorial digits, or unscrupulous enough to make use of fixed ropes.'[2]

The following summer Gross confounded these remarks by climbing his Eliminate 'A'. He summarised the route thus:

'The climb was done in perfect conditions. It is probably QUITE as severe as "B" Eliminate, and is consistently of great exposure. Rubbers are essential; 100 feet of rope.'[3]

Throughout, the route has tremendous position and is sustained at a good standard. Immediately the first ledge is left behind the excitement begins with the rocks falling away to the bed of Great Gully some distance below. The next pitch, taking a technical wall at the point of weakest resistance, is more than a little pushy and I note with some interest Gross's comment here regarding the first ascent:

'Good holds are to be found, and the route goes straight ahead for 15 feet. It is then necessary to make a difficult step to the right; small, good, but not obvious holds enable one to rise on to a ledge, and a good pointed grip is available. A turf ledge must now be attained at shoulder height. Search reveals a hold for the left hand in a vertical crack above the ledge, and this and a press up on the right achieve the desired ledge, and it is then a more simple matter to reach a good grass platform. There is no belay here, but the second man has a good large stance.'[3]

On reaching the famed Rochers Perches

Julia Laverock on Isengard/Samba Pa Ti pulling through the overhang to gain the slab below the cave.

pitch the exposure is nothing less than dramatic, the climbing hard and Gross had the added difficulty of having to contend with some large loose boulders—hence the name. Today's leaders do not have this further fear factor to deal with, the blocks have now entirely gone, but even so the next few feet from the ledge are a somewhat heart-pounding affair. Imagine then Gross's position on this technically difficult pitch, climbing with only rudimentary equipment which meant any slip at all would inevitably spell disaster. He and Basterfield were only half-way up this huge, unclimbed, unknown face of rock. Neither knew if it could be climbed or what lay over the overhangs that threatened above—the psychological barrier must have been immense:

'The crag overhangs to a tremendous extent, and it was decided to work out to the left. The immediate objective is a small ledge at a height of 8 feet, and some 10 feet to the left of the platform. This pitch is extremely exposed, and is a very exacting lead. A start is made on poor sloping footholds, and trust must be placed in some detached blocks which appear to be firm, however. Delicate balance eventually lands one on the ledge, and a further stride to the left gives access to a good ledge leading to a big recess roofed by a great overhang.'[3]

The next two pitches are equally intimidating, if perhaps not quite so hard, and provide plenty of excitement until less serious ground is gained. The last pitch, as described here, is really searching for independence—the most logical finish is up the obvious crack bagged by Gordon and Craig's route. It doesn't really matter a jot at this stage—even the safest way to the summit could not detract from the sheer intoxication of this definitively excellent climb.

Isengard/Samba Pa Ti is a logical and tremendous climb of some difficulty that evolved in stages. I remember tackling the wall of Isengard, now rated 5b, when it was only graded Hard Very Severe—it seemed reasonable for that grade! But that was back in the days when there were really only two grades of climb—those you could do and those you couldn't! It is a steep, absorbing pitch with an exciting pull through the overlap at the top of the wall.

Do the route in the sun if possible because cold fingers will make a difference. This means from mid-morning to mid-afternoon in summer—climbing a fingery or strenuous route on windy Dow without sunshine can be a rather masochistic experience. Even so, despite its sometimes cold nature, the rock is rough and clean, dries quickly, and does not have a propensity for lichen as do many other Lakeland crags.

The merely vertical technicalities of the first section, the wall to the big cave of Eliminate 'A', are thrown into splendid contrast by the obscenely overhanging roof of the distinct second half. Get the protection sorted out before you go. It's very easy to kick it off as you pass with legs swinging wildly as you cut loose and power through the first roof. Above this it doesn't appear to relent, a veritable sea of bulging rock awaits. But if tackled in stages—keep moving on the steep bits then rest before tackling the next bulge—it is quite reasonable. This logical combination of Isengard/Samba Pa Ti gives a route very much in the modern idiom—with solid climbing placing it well in its grade. Go for it.

1. 1943 *Journal of the Fell & Rock Climbing Club*—'Obituary to H. S. Gross' by G. Basterfield.
2. 1922 Guidebook published by The Fell & Rock Climbing Club—*Dow Crag* by George S. Bower.
3. 1923 *Journal of the Fell & Rock Climbing Club*—'Climbs Old & New—Eliminate "A"' by H. S. Gross.

Julia Laverock on the slab stance of Eliminate 'A' at the end of the first pitch with streamers clouding the sky and the white quartz slab of Giant's Crawl beyond.

DOW CRAG: Giant's Crawl

GIANT'S CRAWL: 420ft (128m), Difficult.
First Ascent: E. T. W. Addyman, D. T. Addyman, Stobart, April 1909.
Location: 'B' Buttress, Dow Crag, Coniston.

Giant's Crawl—Summary

Following a diagonal slabby ramp from left to right, rising from Great Gully and crossing the upper section of 'B' Buttress, the line couldn't be more obvious. Start immediately right of the foot of the gully.

1. 60ft (18m). Take the easy slabs to move left along a narrow ledge to the foot of a crack.

2. 80ft (24m). Follow the crack for 30ft (9m) then continue up the great quartz-speckled slab to a rock ledge on the edge. Move up to the right to reach belays.

3. 30ft (9m). Continue easily up for a few feet then climb the slab on the left to another ledge and small belays.

4. 90ft (27m). Take the slabs above following a central line and passing ledges with poor belays. A large grass ledge overlooking Easy Terrace is reached (it is possible to escape off here by traversing down the right to reach the Terrace).

5. 40ft (12m). Traverse along the ledge to reach an overhanging corner.

6. 60ft (18m). Climb the awkward crack up the corner to a good ledge. Walk round to the left to another crack in a steep groove, this has better holds and leads to a belay on the right.

7. 60ft (18m). Easy climbing and then scrambling leads to the top.

Giant's Crawl—Description

There are few climbing crags finer than Dow. To anyone passing along the path below it creates an impact that couldn't be heightened by any artist's impression. In all, five tall rock buttresses tower above a steep scree slope which in turn increases the dramatic effect by plunging directly into the copper blue-black Goat's Water. To the climber the crag looks naked, clean and inviting—immaculate rock made for climbing. On closer acquaintance it proves to be, if anything, even better than it looks. Hidden in the whole, each separate buttress has its own distinct character and within this enough climbing intrigue to last the most ardent admirer a lifetime.

The buttresses are named 'A', 'B', 'C', 'D' and 'E' in order from left to right. On the far left 'A' is the most independent, 'B'—on which lies Giant's Crawl—the largest and most complex and 'C' the one whose toe forms the lowest point of the whole crag. Goat's Water, a water of many moods, lies below the crag in the bottom of this hanging valley. Opposite Dow the mighty Old Man guards the sanctuary, preserving its solitude. However from the summit of Dow, when the climbing day is won, a wonderfully panoramic view to the south, to the sea and to the wilder heights of Scafell in the north, and Helvellyn in the east adds yet another dimension to a day already blessed.

The route is aptly named, for what appears from some distance below to be a thin line traversing the face is in fact a good slab of more than ample proportions. It is a most attractive climb taking in rock that is often coated in pure white quartz—indeed it is the quartz that often provides the frequent and generous holds. It winds its way from bottom to top in the best of mountaineering traditions and whilst the climbing is quite moderate in difficulty it is none-the-less continually interesting in situations of tremendous exposure.

Aesthetically and spiritually it would be hard to better Giant's Crawl within the category of Difficult and it makes for a good route for beginner and veteran alike. It says something of its bold-looking initial appearance that it was some twenty-one years after the first ascent of Dow, that of Great Gully by a large party including W. P. Haskett-Smith in

At the flake stance on Ordinary Route 'C' with the scree of Goat's Water tarn below.

16

Climbing the white quartz slab of Giant's Crawl.

1888, before this comparatively mild route was actually climbed. Perhaps the best way to capture the full flavour of this climb would be to ascend it at a leisurely pace in boots and with rucksack filled with flask and sandwiches en route to the other classics, Bowfell Buttress (above Langdale) and Moss Ghyll (on Scafell). That would be some great day out on the hills and, naturally, would have to be started early by walking from Coniston!

DOW CRAG: Ordinary Route 'C'

ORDINARY ROUTE 'C': 360ft (110m), Difficult.
First Ascent: G. F. Woodhouse, A. J. Woodhouse, August 1904.
Location: 'C' Buttress, Dow Crag, Coniston.

Ordinary Route 'C'—Summary

'C' Buttress forms the lowest point of the crag and this well-worn climb starts just left of this. Although the following description is a logical way to tackle this climb the pitches can be split in a number of ways and there are a number of variations in line that are no less worthy.

1. 50ft (15m). Up to gain the blunt nose of the buttress to a narrow ledge at the top of a flake.

2. 55ft (17m). Climb to a small ledge and take the smooth scoop above to ledges. A good ledge with a flake offers the best stance and belay.

3. 70ft (21m). Move up from the left end of the ledge to climb the slab rightwards then move easily leftwards to a ledge on the edge of the buttress.

4. 70ft (21m). Take the corner above and ascend rightwards up the slab to a ledge and a better ledge and belay just above this.

5. 45ft (14m). Take the obvious traverse left to the crack and climb the wall on its left. Move over to a cave and climb the crack on its left to gain the top of the flake. Step left then right to a belay some 10 (3m) above the flake.

6. 65ft (20m). Cross the slabs on the right to a ledge and continue along a gangway round a bulge to another ledge. A short wall to the left and then a horizontal traverse leads to Easy Terrace.

Ordinary Route 'C'—Description

The first thing you realise, on arrival at the crag, is that the blue tent you see from Goat's Water is in fact an aluminium rescue box. Whilst it should be left strictly alone it marks the usual and logical place to dump the rucksack, eat the sandwiches and enjoy the sunshine. A little way to the right, around the corner of the buttress, is a spring of fresh clear mountain water issuing straight out of solid rock—I have never known it to dry up and it slakes many a fearsome thirst. The buttress itself is the line of our route and it gives an excellent introduction to this large and interesting crag.

It is a deservedly popular route of some length, its open nature offering a chance to enjoy the surrounding mountain vista.

However it shouldn't be underestimated for its slabby nature means that it can be quite tricky if at all wet or 'green'. A wary eye should also be kept open for stonefall dislodged by other parties above. Whilst nut runners can be placed almost at will it is still useful to take a couple of longish tape slings for there are a number of excellent flake belays.

Bower's first guidebook to the crag introduced the route in a way that captures the relaxed nature of this popular route:

'Ordinary Route—Moderate; any number of patient climbers, who may smoke before, during, and after each pitch . . .'[1]

Once the route is commenced, height is quickly gained and with it a delightful view begins to unfold. Far below, the coffin-shaped Goat's Water can be anything from sinister black to translucent blue. Black when an angry wind ruffles the surface and many is the climber on Dow who has seen sudden savage gusts of wind lift whole slabs of water, turning them into clouds of spray. Blue when the submerged boulders are seen through a mirror-calm surface, for they take on the colour of turquoise. This is a result of the copper rich veins hereabouts. The heart of the Old Man must be virtually hollow from the activities of centuries of mining, and green copper ore can be found in the rocks at a number of localities on Dow.

A good examination can also be made of the impressive-looking chimney crack to the left. First climbed by the incredible O. G. Jones in 1897 it was a formidable route for its day and was done whilst he was on his way to climb on Scafell! Not only did he bag this frightening-looking chimney, after arriving by train and walking all the way from Coniston that morning, but he went on to climb on Scafell the same day and descended to the Wastdale Head Inn in time to enjoy his evening meal. No wonder he explained his initials O. G. stood for 'Only Genuine', for Jones was some unique character. (His full story is told in my book *Lakeland's Greatest Pioneers*, Robert Hale, 1983.)

Once Ordinary Route 'C' is completed, a safe descent made along and down Easy Terrace, and a few tales swopped over a well earned lunch by the rescue box, thoughts will turn to other climbs. Apart from those de-

Geneu,éve Lubas on Ordinary Route 'C'.

Climbing rib of Ordinary Route 'C' with the rescue box visible bottom left.

scribed here why not try the Central Chimney at Severe or if you are feeling good then Murray's Route commencing up the V-chimney, just behind the box, is another superb Severe.

If you are a newcomer you should not feel outfaced by this large cliff. You have the whole of Dow to explore, all those tremendous routes to discover, countless days of adventure, sunshine and rain to look forward to—cherish these formative days; they may be the best days of your life.

1. 1922 *Fell & Rock Climbing Club Guide*—'Dow Crag' by George S. Bower.

THE CONISTON FELLS—WALLOWBARROW

WALLOWBARROW: Thomas.
Map Ref: SD 222967 (Named Low Crag by Ordnance Survey).
Guidebooks: *Rock Climbing in the Lake District* by Birkett, Cram, Eilbeck and Roper. *Scafell, Dow & Eskdale* (FRCC Guide) by Al Phizacklea.
Attitude: Faces south-west.
Altitude: 900ft (270m).
Rock: Rhyolite—slightly polished.
Access: From High Wallowbarrow Farm (small charge for parking) take the track through the farmyard up to the crag (10 minutes).

Alternatively take the scenic track starting by the little church at Seathwaite (25 minutes).
Descent: To the left.
Observations: The crag is made up of two main buttresses, the West and the East, with a number of smaller outcrops dotted around the area. The West and East Buttresses are separated by a large vegetated gully—known as Red Gully—with the West Buttress situated on the left immediately above the approach track from the farm. Thomas climbs the West Buttress.

Wallowbarrow

THOMAS: 190ft (58m), Severe (Hard).
First Ascent: W. F. Dowlen, D. Stroud, 26 June 1955.
Location: West Buttress, Wallowbarrow Crag, Dunnerdale.

Thomas—Summary

The west buttress lies just above the track and on the right at its lowest point is an oak tree. The climb takes the clean rib just left of this.

1. 130ft (40m). Climb the groove in the rib, rather polished, to a steep wall capped by some blocks. Step right beneath these and pull steeply over to a ledge. From the left gain cracks in the wall and climb steeply, with good spike runner, until the difficulty eases and a large ledge which tops the rib is reached. Block belay.

2. 60ft (18m). Go right for a few feet only to the foot of an obvious shallow groove. Another steep wall leads to the groove and the crux is constituted by reaching the unique little pinnacle (!) at its top. Nut belays well back.

Thomas—Description

Between the rugged red granite of Eskdale and the darker, smoother, more familiar rhyolites of the Coniston fells the attractions of Wallowbarrow and quiet Dunnerdale are many. Its charming, elfin-like position above the oaks, silver birch and bracken, is suitably matched by the climbing quality on the fine rocks of the West and East Buttresses. Not too far away, through the woods and across neatly stone-walled fields, the young river Duddon splashes through a rocky gorge where further climbing interest can be found. Excellent routes with plenty of interest and length abound up to the Very Severe category. What's more they dry quickly.

The traditionally mixed deciduous woods of this quiet valley make it a must for anyone who appreciates this type of apparently unordered peaceful beauty. During autumn the colours can be breathtaking and the climbing, because of the crag's friendly nature, perfect for that time of the year. The quickest

Tony Greenbank beginning the crux moves of the last pitch on Thomas.

WALLOW BARROW
WEST BUTTRESS

RED GULLY

belay point

THOMAS

approach is through the farmyard (remember to close all the gates) and this is pleasant enough. But for those with a little time on their hands the approach from either Seathwaite Church or the Newfield Inn, eventually crossing the bridge over the Wallowbarrow Gorge, soaks in all the atmosphere of this delightful valley. The inn itself, away from the more popular tourist areas, remains unspoilt and welcoming. Along with a roaring wood fire comes a striking, flow-banded slate floor—unique to Seathwaite. I must confess to ending many an evening's climbing here.

Logically perhaps, one of the very best routes hereabouts was the first route to be pioneered on delightful Wallowbarrow. The premier was climbed by the then Eskdale Outward Bound instructor, Walter Dowlen. He can feel justifiably proud in discovering this rather fine and distinctive climbing area. Despite much speculation as to why this climb was named Thomas—most surmise that it comes from the unique 'John Thomas', a six-inch spike that forms the top handhold

above the final groove—the official derivation is somewhat different. Dowlen says he named the route from the biblical connotation 'doubting Thomas' because:

'When Dacre (wiseacre) Stroud and I did Thomas the final wall was vegetated and fairly well supplied with loose holds. I tried several lines—the groove on the left (now the finish of Perseverance) then further right and finally the successful line. Even this took a couple of oscillations, during the first a handhold snapped off without warning.'[1]

Whatever the source of the name, Thomas is one of those really fine routes. Akin to Little Chamonix on Shepherd's Crag in Borrowdale, Kestrel Wall on Eagle Crag in Grisedale or Creagh Dhu Wall on Tremadog (Wales), it rises to classic status rather unexpectedly. The fact that it isn't placed remotely high or doesn't weave its way up an immense rock wall adds to its enigma. In fact it enhances the climbing quality because it is so surprisingly good.

Wallowbarrow showing the line of Thomas.

Tony Greenbank belaying Al Phizacklea up the first rib.

The line is positive and the rib readily rears to the vertical in a number of places. The first long pitch gives good value. If it is a little damp or if you're off form at the start of a season it can feel both hard and committing. Good! Then comes the second pitch another steep little wall, to gain a slightly-defined bottomless groove. No wonder it was the third option on the first ascent—it is a bit precarious and very exposed. Good line slings can be taken over spikes at leisure on the previous pitch, with an equally good nut alternative nearby. But here the line sling becomes vital as there is little else to protect what, all things being equal, must sensibly be regarded as the technical crux. Positive and confident footwork are essential to balance up successfully and reach the 'John Thomas' spike which marks the end of the difficulties and the top of a fine climb.

I note in my climbing diary that I found the wet first pitch harder than any of the surrounding VSs climbed on the same day and I can only assume that this was because the slightly balancey nature of the climbing, combined with the then lack of nuts, had proved rather intimidating. Certainly on the autumn day that I took these photographs, just as the bracken was reddening and the oaks were turning to gold, Tony Greenbank found the top groove the most problematic. Considerably cheered on grasping 'JT' he reminisced about his earlier days with colleague Dowlen and their early British ascent together of the North Face of the Piz Badile—'Not bad eh youth?'

Not bad at all. Actually, very different. But two good routes—both classics in different ways.

1. *Personal correspondence* by Walter Dowlen/ Tony Greenbank 1987—Tony Greenbank collection.

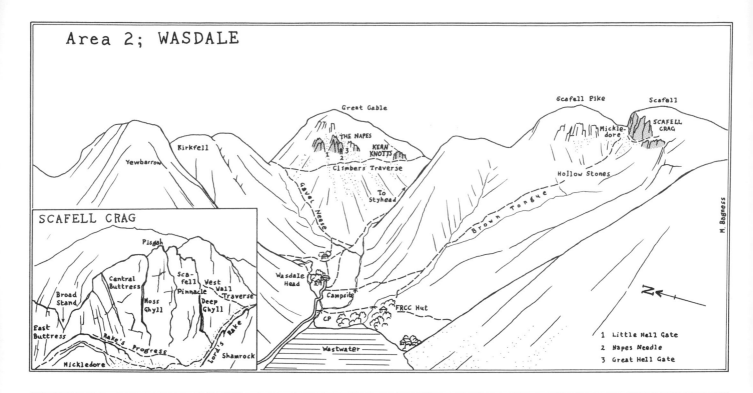

SCAFELL CRAG

1 Little Hell Gate
2 Napes Needle
3 Great Hell Gate

WASDALE—ESK BUTTRESS

ESK BUTTRESS: Bridge's Route, Central Pillar, The Cumbrian.
Map Ref: NY 223064 (shown as Dow Crag on OS map).
Guidebooks: *Rock Climbing in the Lake District* by Birkett, Cram, Eilbeck, Roper. *Scafell, Dow & Eskdale* (FRCC Guide) by Al Phizacklea.
Attitude: Faces south.
Altitude: 1500ft (460m).
Rock: Rhyolite.
Access: It is important to note that although for convenience I have classified this crag in the Wasdale section, it is actually situated on the opposite side of Scafell—in Upper Eskdale. The usual approaches are from Brotherilkeld in Eskdale (limited parking by the telephone kiosk) by a path along the Esk (1.5 hours), or from Cockley Beck by going up Mosedale to descend to Lingcove Beck. This is crossed and from here the hillside is traversed by a path under Gait Crags and then across the bog of the Great Moss and up to the foot of the crag (1.75 hours). Alternatively, the crag can be reached from Wasdale or Borrowdale but both are a bit of a flog.
Descent: Traverse over to the left of the crag, cross a stream and continue down the fellside to contour back beneath the crag.
Observations: The centre section of Esk Buttress takes the form of a magnificent pillar, vertical clean and of perfect rock. It presents one of the most aesthetically inspiring challenges in the district yet remained unclimbed until the 1930s—when Alf Bridge produced the superb Bridge's Route described here.

CENTRAL PILLAR

THE CUMBRIAN

BRIDGES ROUTE

belay point

ESK BUTTRESS: Bridge's Route, Central Pillar, The Cumbrian

Bridges Route, The Cumbrian and
Central Pillar on Esk Buttress.

ESK BUTTRESS: Bridge's Route, Central Pillar and The Cumbrian
BRIDGE'S ROUTE: 265ft (81m), Hard Severe.
First Ascent: A. W. Bridge, A. B. Hargreaves,
M. Linnell, W. S. Dyson, 10 July 1932.
CENTRAL PILLAR: 350ft (107m), E2 (5b).
First Ascent: P. Crew, M. Owen, 17 June 1962.
THE CUMBRIAN: 270ft (82m), E5 (6a).
First Ascent: R. Valentine, P. Braithwaite (alt), 5
May 1974. Free M. & B. Berzins 1977. Pitches 1 &
2 R. Graham, A Hyslop, 1977.
Location: Esk Buttress, Scafell, Upper Eskdale.

Bridge's Route—Summary

About halfway up the scree, where it joins the vegetated bottom slopes of the crag, there are one or two level sections suitable for dumping the sac. Directly above this, up the clean wall, is the line of the route. Scramble up the vegetated rocks to a clean ledge—below and about 30ft (9m) right of a square chimney. In actual fact there is a narrow pillar above, the square chimney defines its left edge and a line of cracks and grooves its right edge. It is the cracks and grooves that form the line of the route.

1. 135ft (41m). Step up and right from the ledge and follow up cracks and grooves, the obvious line of weakness, to a ledge. Take the crack on the left to a ledge. Climb a steep groove, step right and continue to the distinct top of the pillar. Flake belays. It is possible to split this pitch in a number of places.

2. 45ft (14m). Make an exposed traverse horizontally leftwards into a corner groove. Up this for a few feet until possible to exit left and move up to the rock ledge stance.

3. 85ft (26m). Traverse left along the rock ledge to an exposed step leading across a groove and onto a wall. Cross the wall to gain a groove up on the left. Climb this to pull up to a large grassy terrace and belay well back.

Central Pillar—Summary

Start as for Bridge's Route.
1. 135ft (41m). Pitch 1 of Bridge's Route.
2. 70ft (21m), (5a). Take the thin cracks up

the wall above the belay until the traverse line right can be followed. This leads to a steep rock barrier on the right. From good holds at its base climb up leftwards until it is possible to step back right onto a small exposed stance on the rib.

3. 45ft (14m), (5b). Climb the shallow groove to a small ledge on the right. Step back left and up to the overlap that caps the groove. Pull over this onto a slab and move across right to belay in the corner. Old pegs and a block for belays. A poorly protected pitch.

4. 100ft (30m), (5b). Step up and traverse right with the feet on the break. At the end of the break pull up the steep wall to gain a small awkward ledge. There is a hidden peg behind a flake. Gain the stick-out block and pull up on this to gain high handholds. Another few moves are necessary to reach the traverse line leading out to the right. Move along this until it is possible to climb the wall, now easy, to the top.

The Cumbrian—Summary
Start as for Bridge's Route.

1. 100ft (30m), (5a). Follow Bridge's Route to the top of the crack and from the pinnacle ledge step right onto the main wall to climb a thin crack. This is followed for about 30ft (9m) until a step left is made to a continuation crack. Take this to a narrow ledge.

2. 60ft (18m), (5a). Climb the slab above to join the traverse of Central Pillar. Follow this to the small ledge stance on the rib.

3. 110ft (33m), (6a). Move left and climb up to gain an awkward corner below the impending headwall. There are small wire placements here—poor. Step down left and move left into the groove directly below the corner. Move up the crack to an excellent runner (approximately Rock 6) then make a few difficult moves (crux) to gain the rib immediately right of the corner. Step left into the corner and continue up this for 30ft (9m) until a rest can be had. Continue up the corner, over a bulge, and move rightwards to a ledge below the final short section of corner. Continue up this with some awkward moves until a step left and final pull gives the finishing ledge and belay. It is easier to avoid the final corner by pulling out onto the left wall—but this is the soft option.

Easy rocks lead up to the top.

Bridge's Route, Central Pillar and The Cumbrian—Description
If one had to name a favourite Lakeland Crag I think Esk Buttress would be the one on the top of my list. It stands some 300ft (90m) high,

Esk Buttress.

The delicate and exposed traverse left from the pedestal belay on Bridge's Route.

sunburned, climbing this wonderful rock. Even during the last throes of winter, when the snow still smooths white over all below, the red rocks of this buttress are pleasant to the touch.

If I have the choice I always walk in from Cockley Beck. It may not be quite the quickest approach, and it is probably the boggiest, but for the climber who appreciates the natural environment of the high hills I know nothing to beat it. In summer after the green brackens surrounding the track disappear, the open bog of upper Mosedale is best skirted high on the left if wet feet are to be avoided. However on a hot day it's cool wetness may not go unappreciated and a more direct route can be chosen. From here the way becomes more open and the straw-brown hill grasses and rough grey rhyolite boulders predominate.

From the col above Mosedale, you get the first view of Esk Buttress still some considerable distance away. To the right Bowfell, dead ahead Scafell Pike and falling away to the left the bulky shoulder of the Scafell massif. A magnificent and thrilling panorama and at its heart the lure of climbing on Esk Buttress pulling you breathlessly forwards.

The central pillar is the setting for all these climbs. They start from the same point—there the similarity ends. Bridge's Route offers fine open quality climbing in a superb setting. Central Pillar keeps moving right, avoiding the main challenge but at the same time finding superb rock, exposure and sufficient difficulty and verticality to establish it as the model of its grade. The Cumbrian is the line taking the leaning groove scribed up the centre of the final impending headwall. All routes to dream about; before you climb them and afterwards.

Bridge's is a route that can be tackled in most conditions by a party of any size. Although the initial stances are fairly small the belays are excellent and it is no problem to clip on another body somewhere on the stance. By the time you actually start the route the position is already grand and the few hundred feet up the pillar above only improve on this. The rock is superb, absolutely pristine, and the climbing equally fine.

It is steep all the way, with some quite bold difficult sections; but these are confined to a manageable length before a good hold, runner or ledge appears. Confidence thus boosted, you continue again to arrive eventually elated at the broken top of the pillar. Above you the vertical wall looks technical. Above this again

a solid pillar of beautifully clean naked rock, in a wild and untamed mountain setting. There are no roads or buildings to be seen and the clear waters of the Esk are untroubled by pollution. The only noise is that of the natural world; the wind ruffling the cotton grasses of the Great Moss far below, raven or peregrine, the contented baa-ing of the grazing Herdwicks.

On a summer's day it can be almost too hot to climb on this south-facing cliff. There was an occasion, and I swear it's true, when, stripped to nothing but shorts, I got badly

the headwall overhangs somewhat. There is no respite on the sweeping verticality to the right. Across to the left, undercut by a smooth-looking chimney, it is sickeningly exposed. Nevertheless this is the way.

Out across a traverse line which responds to the delicate but positive approach, the first few moves constitute the crux and once you are underway it will be found to be easier than it looks. The chimney is crossed and the large rock ledge on the left provides a wonderful sanctuary from the exposure below.

This is soon found again however when, after traversing leftwards, a few massed flakes lead to an awkward step across a bottomless corner before you gain the finishing wall. A fitting and rewarding end to a route that dares to push up into the heart of the central rock pillar of Esk Buttress.

The possibility of a more direct line up the buttress was investigated and found to be possible in 1962. Tongues loosened on Cumbrian beer divulged the information to the waiting ears of the raiding Welshmen, Crew and Owen. The following morning in the sobriety of a June day the race was on. The Welsh team won with Austin, Metcalf and Soper arriving too late to snatch the plum. They consoled themselves on Red Edge and the aptly named Black Sunday—but there was only one Central Pillar climbed that day.

Despite the fact that the route does not live up to the concept of directly tackling the front face, it does follow a logical line of weakness. Finally it breaks through the top wall after traversing from bottom left to top right. This line of direction maintains the grade at E2 for the direct routes. The Cumbrian, Fall Out and Strontium Dog are all considerably more difficult undertakings than the route ascended in 1962. Hence Central Pillar provides consistently airy climbing—the blueprint of difficulty for the E2 grade.

The initial traverse up and then out from the friendly rocks of Bridge's is pleasant, without real difficulty. Yet by the time you arrive at the awkward stance perched on the rib, you are thoroughly aware of your vulnerability and fly-like position on the wall. The groove above is a natural link through to higher rocks. It is both smooth and bold, capped by an overlap, and the end is always in doubt.

Recalling the first time I climbed this groove is amusing now, but at the time it didn't seem quite so funny. Sometimes there is a peg in a horizontal crack before the final steepening moves to the overlap. There

wasn't on this occasion (neither should there be today with the array of nut wires at your disposal) and I had no runner below. With increasing anxiety I managed to place a tape over a small flaky spike on the right wall. Logically it wouldn't have held much but the psychological relief was significant. With renewed confidence I moved up towards the overlap to search for something above the blankness. Then bridging up higher, placing my left foot out onto the runner flake, it snapped clean off! My only point of protection slid ominously down the rope and into oblivion.

It's funny how, at times like these when you are most committed and the safety net is no longer there, you remain calmest. There is no point in being anything else I suppose. Time seems to go slower, the essential holds appear magically in sequence, and you climb at your best. So it was now. The foot found enough, the balance remained intact and the hands reached high above the barrier to grasp the positive holds above.

Bob Wightman on the beautiful rock of The Cumbrian, on the lower wall of Esk Buttress.

Luke Steer solos the steep final wall on Central Pillar with a few hundred feet of space below.

Louise Dickie pulls from the vertical onto the tremendously exposed slab that ends the second pitch.

It all depends on your personal preferences—that pitch remains my choice for the crux; the next is much more my style. After a traverse right, especially awkward for the tall, it is just plain thuggery and long reaches up the hanging wall. This tilted shield of rock is remarkably positioned, and what is lost in finesse is more than made up for by its brutal honesty. There is a hidden peg on a small ledge and although it is old, not many will pass it by without clipping. From this ledge the top of a large stick out block is reached. This must be fully utilised to gain holds high on the steep wall above. It's been there a long time, many have used it, most place a tape sling around it, but use it gently for on close examination it does look somewhat rickety. However, this is no place to linger.

The pull from the block is possibly physically the most difficult section of the route, but it is short and good holds soon appear. A traverse right and then easier climbing up a rib leads to the top of this particularly grand buttress. There is now space and time to take off the boots and reflect on the intricacies of the last few hundred feet.

For those interested in the most difficult and challenging routes, there could be no more aesthetically inspiring line than the precariously poised corner of The Cumbrian. Perhaps it's wrong to call it a corner. This name implies a certain gentility and a feeling of security. In actual fact it is not a right angle with both walls vertical but a leaning corner; a three-dimensional reality overhanging in every plane—a corner inverted with one wall now the sloping roof and the other the impending wall. Some corner!

Some line. In physical reality it is the most magnificent and challenging feature cutting the headwall. From below (and it is visible from afar) it is a route that just defies you to climb it. And carefully note that even within the drama of its big wall and high mountain setting, the product is not belied by its wrapping. You must be ready and prepared for its difficulty.

The worst bit is actually starting. After preliminary ground you arrive at the impending headwall and here the small wire runners do nothing to instil confidence. (They are rubbish!) Moves to the left to find the groove,

comparatively hidden from your side position, seem too prematurely awkward for you are not yet even in sight of the corner above. Persistence unlocks the sequence and then the groove conceives a runner. Positive holds move you to a really bomb-proof nut (approx. Rock 6) which can be placed at a stretch. It is perfectly positioned for the next few moves constitute the crux. Surprisingly you find yourself moving up the wall just right of the corner. There are some good, if small, flake holds before you balance back into the groove. It is now possible to use the left foot on the wall where good footholds occur at regular intervals. The position remains strenuous and runners in the groove are disappointingly awkward to place.

The crack in the corner is one of those that seems to thwart every nut you are carrying. Even when the struggle is won and a runner placed, it does nothing to inspire confidence. Unless you are very strong it may be better to press on to the good rest available (some 30ft (9m) above) relying on the excellent nut below the crux. This was my technique, laying up the edge and enjoying the excellence of the footholds as they occurred. However it is necessary to pace yourself confidently. A fall in these circumstances hardly bears contemplating. Luke Steer exploring the opportunity of every likely nut placement hung unruffled as I photographed him. Some people are too strong by half!

Various grades have been given to this climb but I believe the E5 6a tag to be the most realistic. The crux is technical and powerful, but it is relatively short and, in my opinion, no single move reaches the 6b category. Afterwards the climbing eases technically but not physically. There is no rest for some 30ft (9m) after the crux and above this there is plenty more climbing.

I suppose after meeting the challenge of such a climb you can feel confident that you have arrived in the E5 category. There again, actually to climb a route like this in the first place—you know it already.

.Despite the excellence of these three selected routes, the choice is almost unimportant when climbing on Esk. Only start when the bracken drips the dew and finish in the moonlight.

Labels on image: Sphinx Rock · Little Hell Gate · Gable Traverse · Gavel Neese · The Dress Circle · EAGLE'S NEST RIDGE DIRECT · NAPES NEEDLE · Great Hell Gate · To Kern Knotts · O belay point

WASDALE—THE NAPES

THE NAPES: Napes Needle, Eagle's Nest Ridge Direct.
Map Ref: NY 211099.
Guidebooks: *Rock Climbing in the Lake District* by Birkett, Cram, Eilbeck, Roper. *Great Gable* (FRCC Guide) by P. Fearnehough.
Attitude: Faces south-west.
Altitude: 2,250ft (685m).
Rock: Rhyolite—very polished.
Access: From Wasdale (car park on the green before Wasdale Head Inn or from the Inn) there are two main approaches. The more direct takes the steep shoulder of Gavel Neese directly to the end of the crags and the other traverses across from the top of Sty Head Pass (as for the approach to Kern Knotts). In either case follow the track up towards Sty Head. After a bridge over the beck falling from Beck Head is crossed, a steep path branches directly up the south-west shoulder of Great Gable. This is Gavel Neese and can be followed until you are level with the foot of the Napes crass from where a traverse across scree picks up a track (Gable Traverse) beneath the crags. For the uninitiated it can be difficult to find the correct height to traverse and an easier and more straightforward approach is from the top of Sty Head Pass. From here follow the Great Gable track for a few hundred yards until a path traverses out left. Follow this first under Kern Knotts then on to cross the large scree shoot of Great Hell Gate (Tophet Wall stands high on the left side of this), eventually to arrive at the 'back' of Napes Needle. Contour around beneath this, then ascend to deposit the gear in the Dress Circle up to the left of the Needle (1 hour).
Descent: From the top of Eagle's Nest Ridge Direct it is best to traverse left to descend a scree gully known as Little Hell Gate to reach the Gable Traverse. To descend from the Dress Circle (bottom of the Needle) continue along the path (Gable Traverse) to squeeze through a rock cleft and then pass under the Sphinx Rock to reach the shoulder of Gavel Neese.
Observations: The sunny disposition and rough clean rock of these rugged crags have maintained their popularity ever since the ascent of Napes Needle over one hundred years ago (an event generally recognised as the birth of rock climbing). The ridges, aretes and pinnacles provide the definitive classic climbing ground.

The Great Gable showing the routes up Nape's Needle and Eagle's Nest Ridge Direct.

THE NAPES: Napes Needle and Eagle's Nest Ridge Direct

The moon over Wastwater, seen from Gavel Neese descending after a climbing day on the Napes crags of Great Gable.

NAPES NEEDLE: 55ft (17m), Very Difficult.
First Ascent: W. P. Haskett-Smith (solo), June 1886.
EAGLE'S NEST RIDGE DIRECT: 165ft (50m), Mild Very Severe (4a).
First Ascent: G. A. Solly, W. C. Slingsby, G. P. Baker, W. A. Brigg, 15 April 1892.
Location: The Napes, Great Gable.
Map Ref: NY 211099.

Napes Needle—Summary

Start beneath the large crack that faces Wasdale (The Wasdale Crack).

1. 40ft (12m). Traverse out to the edge and follow it to a shoulder and belay below the top block. (Alternatively the Wasdale Crack provides an entertaining and polished thrutch.)

2. 15ft (5m). From the right corner mantleshelf onto the small ledge. From a standing position foot traverse left until moves can be made up to the flat top. Belay by looping the rope underneath the nose below. The last man can be protected in descent by running the rope under the nose and over the top block.

Eagle's Nest Ridge Direct— Summary

Up to the left of the Needle, immediately left and above the Dress Circle, is a fine arete. This is the line and the route starts from its left edge.

1. 165ft (50m), (4a). Move up diagonally rightwards to find a ledge to the right of the nose (after 50ft (15m)). Step back left to the edge and follow it directly passing the ledges of the Eagle's Nest and then, 15ft (5m) higher, the Crow's Nest. Continue up the edge and maintain this line to the top.

Napes Needle and Eagle's Nest Ridge Direct—Description

To many the valley of Wasdale is a very precious place which, despite its relative popularity retains an air of remoteness. The sudden contrast of the flat plain, lake and field, with the steep flanks of the surrounding fells could hardly be more dramatic. The tall fells of Yewbarrow, Pillar, Kirkfell, Great

Gable, Lingmell, Scafell Pike and Scafell all circle its head, and as they rise high above the few trees, above the bracken, above the gorse, their softness rears into hard rock. Here lies the select world of the mountaineer and hillsman and, quite fittingly, the birthplace of rock climbing.

There are no hills like the Wasdale hills,
When Spring comes up the dale,
Nor any woods like the Larch Woods
Where the primroses blow pale;
And the shadows flicker quiet-wise,
On the stark ridge of Black Sail.[1]

The Napes crags perched seductively on the south-west flanks of Great Gable provide one of the pleasantest climbing grounds in Lakeland. The combination of sunshine, classic rock, and the view across the diminutive patchwork fields mosaicked by the proliferation of stone walls, all add to its friendly disposition. The crag won many hearts during the formative days of rock climbing and indeed the ascent of Napes Needle is regarded as the symbolic birth of the sport.

The Needle is tremendously evocative. Despite its modest height it stands with head erect and chin jutting proudly over an elegant body. Above soar the craggy rocks of the Napes and Needle Ridge and below plunge the running screes that constitute the lower flanks of Great Gable. Detached and distant, its summit can only be gained by the all-out commitment of putting hands to rock and climbing.

With its first ascent, all pretensions were gone of fellwalking grace, of mountaineering in a grand cause to put trophy stylishly under boot. This was not mountaineering but mucking in directly with danger, roughing it with rock scraping skin and stuffing dirt behind the nails, an intoxicating wallow into pure adventure without precedent. The spirit had been freed—rock climbing was born.

I think Haskett-Smith felt rebellious when he released that energy to climb rock, which had been born naturally within him. He had surveyed the Needle before and had settled for the acceptable nature of the Needle Ridge behind. This could be put down to the fact that it actually led somewhere, from the path of Gable Traverse to the top of the Napes Crags. It was of some use, it was within the bounds of convention; stretching them perhaps but excusable. But with the Needle there could be no explanations. Reaching the top had no legitimate purpose whatsoever.

But it was there. It stood, it excited. In the end he could resist it no longer. Alone, free from any restraining voice of conventionality—'Would a Swiss Guide attempt a thing like that?'—he returned.

'Continuing down into the gap and now warmed by exertion, I forgot my headache and began to examine the Needle itself. A deep crack offered a very obvious route for the first stage, but the middle portion of this crack was decidedly difficult, being at that time blocked with stones and turf, all of which has since been cleared away. Many capable climbers were afterwards turned back when trying to make the second ascent not by the sensational upper part but by this lower and (under present conditions) very simple piece.

'From the top of the crack there is no trouble to reach the shoulder, whence the final stage may be studied at ease. The summit is near, being as they say in trans-atlantic cities "only two blocks away," but those same blocks are set one upon the other and the stability of the top one looks very doubtful. My first care was to get two or three stones and test the flatness of the summit by seeing whether anything thrown up could be induced to lodge. If it did, that would be an indication of a moderately flat top, and would hold out hopes of the edge being found not too much rounded to afford a good grip for the fingers. Out of three missiles one consented to stay, and thereby encouraged me to start, feeling as small as a mouse climbing a milestone.'[2]

Haskett-Smith took what is now called the Wasdale Crack and it is a highly strenuous struggle. I personally prefer to move out right and climb the delectable and superbly exposed arete to the shoulder below the top block. From here the fun begins and the climbing is very exposed, bold, balancey and alarmingly polished.

'Between the upper and lower blocks, about five feet up, there is a ragged horizontal chink large enough to admit the toes, but the trouble is to raise the body without intermediate footholds. It seemed best to work up at the extreme right, where the corner projects a little, though the fact that you are hanging over the deep gap makes it a rather "nervy" proceeding. For anyone in a standing position at the corner it is easy to shuffle the feet sideways to the other end of the chink, where it is found that the side of the top block facing outwards is decidedly less vertical. Moreover, at the foot of this side there appeared to my great joy a protuberance which, being covered with lichenous growth, looked as if it might prove slippery, but was placed in the precise spot where it would be most useful in shortening the formidable stretch up to the top edge. Gently and cautiously transferring my weight, I reached up with my right hand and at last was able to feel the edge and prove it to be, not smooth and rounded as it might have been, but a flat and satisfactory grip. My first thought on reaching the top was one of regret

Facing page:
On the top of The Needle. Now to get down! Note the crack which detaches the top block from the rest of The Needle.

that my friends should have missed by a few hours such a day's climbing, three new things and all good; my next one was one of wonder whether getting down again would not prove far more awkward than getting up!

'Hanging by the hands and feeling with the toes for the protuberance provided an anxious moment, but the rest went easily enough, though it must be confessed that it was an undoubted satisfaction to stand once more on solid ground below and look up at my handerchief fluttering in the breeze.'[2]

So the deed was done. Remember Haskett-Smith as you mantleshelf up onto the four-inch ledge on the right edge and then ponderously foot traverse left onto the face of the top block. It remains great stuff and is no push-over. Pay heed to the status of this block—it is completely detached and can be gently rocked from side to side!

The other route I have chosen here is Eagle's Nest Ridge Direct—an outstanding route for its antiquity. It's extremely bold and balancey and of course in 1892 was completely protectionless. The technical grade of 4a may be a little optimistic in super-sticky boots but in anything less than perfect conditions I don't think you will want to quibble unduly. In the early days it had a justifiably high reputation for difficulty which is not surprising when you know it was only the third real rock climb to be done on Great Gable. In fact there have been a number of fatal falls from the arete and there is still little in the way of runners.

I have described the route as one pitch. You need long ropes but the lonely feeling is traditional and enhances the situation on the edge. Alternatively, before the hardest section, it is possible to belay on the good ledge at 50ft (15m).

The last time I climbed on the Napes rocks of Great Gable I descended as the black arms of the Screes and Yewbarrow cradled Wast-water's burnt red. Above the sky graduated from blue to gold and a new moon hung dead centre. With one shot left I held my breath and steadied the camera on my knees.

I will go back to the hills again,
When the day's work is done,
And set my hands against the rocks,
Warm with an April sun,
And see the night creep down the fells,
And the stars climb one by one.[1]

1. 'I Will Go Back', poem by May Wedderburn Cannan from *In War Time*, B. H. Blackwell 1917.
2. 'The First Ascent of Napes Needle' by W. P. Haskett-Smith, 1914 *Journal of the Fell and Rock Climbing Club*.

WASDALE—KERN KNOTTS

KERN KNOTTS: Kern Knotts Crack, Innominate Crack, Buttonhook Route.
Map Ref: NY 216094.
Guidebooks: *Rock Climbing in the Lake District* by Birkett, Cram, Eilbeck and Roper. *Great Gable* (FRCC Guide) by P. Fearnehough.
Attitude: Although generally the crag faces south-west the wall taken by the crack routes (at right angles) faces south-east.
Altitude: 2,000ft (600m).
Rock: Rhyolite.
Access: From Wasdale (car park on the green before the Wasdale Head Inn) follow the track up to the top of Sty Head (the top of the pass connecting Wasdale to Seathwaite in Borrowdale). Then follow up the Great Gable track until, after a few hundred yards a path contours horizontally leftwards across the fellside. After about five minutes from the head of the pass the distinctive clean wall of Kern Knotts Crack comes into sight. The path takes you directly to it (0.75 hour). The approach from Seathwaite in Borrowdale is equally enjoyable and only slightly longer.
Descent: All three routes terminate at the top of Kern Knotts Crack. One can continue to the top by a well worn route (Kern Knotts Chimney) of Difficult standard—this passes under the jammed block and then up the slab above. The best descent from the top of the crag is over to the left (west), or by descending the Kern Knotts Chimney—this is the other side of the same rift of Kern Knotts Crack.
Observations: Despite its small scale the steep nature of Kern Knotts ensures much technical interest. The routes detailed are all significant landmarks of their period and even with the benefit of modern day equipment they offer a challenge that will not be found lacking.

KERN KNOTTS

Sentry Box

INNOMINATE CRACK

KERN KNOTTS CRACK

BUTTONHOOK ROUTE
(Base obscured)

belay point

Kern Knotts and Innominate Crack on Kern Knotts.

KERN KNOTTS: Kern Knotts Crack, Innominate Crack and Buttonhook Route

Leaving the sentry box on Kern Knotts Crack.

KERN KNOTTS CRACK: 70ft (21m), Mild Very Severe (4a).
First Ascent: O. G. Jones, H. C. Bowen, 28 April 1897.
INNOMINATE CRACK: 60ft (18m), Very Severe (4b).
First Ascent: G. S. Bower, Bentley Beetham, J. B. Wilton, 9 April 1921.
BUTTONHOOK ROUTE: 100ft (30m), Hard Very Severe (5a).
First Ascent: F. G. Balcombe, C. J. A. Cooper, June 1934.
Location: Kern Knotts, Great Gable.

Kern Knotts Crack—Summary

Takes the left-hand chimney crack splitting the Sty Head face of the crag.

1. 70ft (21m), (4a). Climb the crack easily to the sentry box (traditional belay). Either take the crack directly (strenuous and awkward) or step onto the right wall (delicate) to climb to the upper section of the crack. Follow the crack, now considerably easier, to the top.

Innominate Crack—Summary

Takes the thin crack on the right.

1. 60ft (18m), (4b). Holds lead to a niche. For a few moves holds in the left-hand thin crack arc used until one can transfer rightwards to the main crack. This is followed to the top.

Buttonhook Route—Summary

This takes the nose of the buttress left of the wall. Start from the lowest point of the crag.

1. 100ft (30m), (5a). Twin cracks lead to the overhang. Pull over, good wedged flake hold up and out to the right, and continue to a small stance (possible belay). The climbing now becomes increasingly delicate. Move left, passing a thread runner, to gain a shallow scoop. Climb this on sloping holds to a ledge with a pinnacle on the right. Continue up the nose to the top of Kern Knotts Crack.

Kern Knotts Crack, Innominate Crack and Buttonhook Route —Description

Despite its brevity, Kern Knotts is a very attractive crag. It has a pleasing aspect, getting a lot of sunshine, and the rock is absolutely excellent—steep and clean. In their day all three of the routes described here were regarded as test-pieces and, although climbing standards have moved on radically, they remain as entertaining and enjoyable little climbs.

The Sty Head face is very nicely clean cut and stands plumb vertical. Despite the smoothness of the rock the holds are extremely positive. On its left edge, effectively forming the nose between this face and the Wasdale face of the crag, lies the challenge of the Buttonhook Route. On the upper part of this climb the holds are by no means large and much of the climbing relies on the frictional qualities of the rock. Fortunately the rhyolite here is somewhat greyer and rougher than on the Sty Head face. However a generation of nailed boot devotees have noticeably smoothed the rugosities and caution should be exercised in wet or damp conditions.

Back in the late 1800s the challenge of something as completely vertical as Kern Knotts Crack needed someone with special qualities to take it on. For the man who, reputedly, could do a one-arm, three-finger pull up—whilst at the same time lifting another climber in the crook of his other arm—it would seem to be no contest. So it proved and O. G. Jones knocked it off in 1897.

On close scrutiny it appears that the apparent non-competitive early nature of rock climbing was in fact a myth. One could go a stage further and say that, on careful examination of the evidence, O. G. Jones was in many ways the ultimate competitor. For after first climbing the route he took to soloing it, reversing down Kern Knotts Chimney and running back round to the bottom. He timed the circuit, completed in something like seven minutes, and issued a challenge for anyone to beat it. I don't believe anyone did.

Despite the performances of Jones all those years ago do not underestimate the severity of this route. The direct way straight up from the sentry box is quite a brutal and precarious thrutch. It defeats many a climber. Whilst the way up the right wall is preferable for those who enjoy delicate balance climbing it is bold and mildly protectionless. All in all it is a route worthy of its reputation.

In the corner, to the right of the clean wall there was once a massive jammed block. A route known as Sepulchre laybacked up its edge for 30ft (10m) and then belayed on the

top of it. Unfortunately, after the earthquake that shook most of northern England in 1980, it decided to move. The shattered debris of this once famous feature now marks the bottom of Innominate Crack. The remains offer a comfortable block belay on which to recline as the leader struggles with the verticality above.

Despite its apparent directness, the thin crack of Innominate is surprisingly technical. It involves intricate bridging and a number of jamming techniques. But it's a great joy to climb and if you are feeling particularly traditional then forget all the nut runners you can so obviously place at will and carry only a couple of line slings. Doing this will heighten the intensity of the experience and re-establish the full meaning of the 1921 ascent. Just don't fall off, that's all!

Buttonhook may have been named after the device used to thread the runners. With modern equipment use of such a tool is no longer necessary, but even so the second half of the climb remains a bold piece of climbing. Balcombe had a meteoric climbing career. An

Looking to Kern Knotts and on down to the Wasdale Head.

Sean Tomlinson in Kern Knotts Crack.

36

Above:
High on Innominate Crack.

Right:
The tricky crux of Buttonhook Route.

innovative and radical cave diver at the inception of the sport, he apparently had but one week's climbing in the Lake District. During those few days of June 1934 he put up, amongst others, the Direct Finish to Central Buttress on Scafell, Engineer's Slabs and Buttonhook Route—some of the most difficult and daring routes of the era!

The start, passing the overhang, is technically the most difficult section of the route. A long reach helps; alternatively undercutting the roof makes it possible for those not so long in the leg. But whatever method is employed, there are not many who will pass this point without giving it some thought. Some, indeed, may not pass it at all. A steep crack leads up to a small stance and this gives a break to be taken before the upper section.

Traversing out left and then up the rib is a delicate affair and for such a small crag the exposure is quite remarkable. The front nose of this buttress requires a cool, steady approach. Despite the sloping nature of the holds the rock is impeccable and offers a really fine piece of climbing. All the routes described here provided a major challenge at the time of their inception. Today, although their psychological impact may be considerably lessened, the actual physical difficulty is just as acute and the climbing, on this delightful outcrop above the valley of Wasdale, every bit as enjoyable as it always was.

WASDALE—EAST BUTTRESS OF SCAFELL

EAST BUTTRESS OF SCAFELL: Mickledore Grooves, Lost Horizons, Great Eastern by the Yellow Slab.
Map Ref: NY 210068.
Guidebooks: *Rock Climbing in the Lake District* by Birkett, Cram, Eilbeck, Roper. *Scafell, Dow & Eskdale* (FRCC Guide) by Al Phizacklea.
Attitude: The crag initially faces south-east, veering further south as it moves around the hillside from Mickledore.
Altitude: 2,700ft (820m).
Rock: Rhyolite, good but lichenous in places.
Access: The quickest, most direct approach is from Wasdale. From the car park at the head of the lake, near the campsite entrance, a well defined track leads up by Lingmell Beck until a steep rib is reached. This is known as Brown Tongue and is followed into the recess of Hollow Stones. Ascend again, passing a large boulder to the combe below Scafell Crag up on the right. Keep directly up the scree at the head of the combe to gain the spur of Mickledore which connects Scafell Pike to Scafell and which separates the East Buttress to the left from Scafell Crag to the right (1.5 hours). It is quite usual to gear-up here because the descent arrives, down Broad Stand, back onto Mickledore.
Descent: This is the same for all the routes. Traverse right across the top of the East Buttress to find a short chimney into a rock-filled gully (Mickledore Gully). Take care not to dislodge any stones. Cross this to join the well marked scrambling route down. This is known as Broad Stand (the walker's route up Scafell) and involves some rocks of Moderate difficulty near the bottom before the Mickledore spur is gained. Mickledore is reached, not at its crest but a little way down its Eskdale flank—through a rock cleft behind a large detached boulder.
Observations: The cliffs of Scafell form a giant horseshoe with the spur of Mickledore dividing them into two sections. The Scafell Crag lies to the right of Mickledore, on the Wasdale side, and the East Buttress to its left, on the Eskdale side. The East Buttress is a large, considerably overhanging, barrel-shaped crag—traditionally the hard man's playground. The climbs are described from right to left, in order of approach from Mickledore, and they increase in height in the same direction.

Despite the southerly aspect of the cliffs their altitude should not be forgotten and they can drip and weep water sometimes all summer. However the routes selected here can generally be expected to dry as quickly as any. The undercut and overhanging nature of the rock and its position on a steep hillside make it one of the most respected climbing grounds in the Lake District.

The morning sun lights up the East Buttress to perfection. The spur of Mickledore is to the right.

MICKLEDORE GROOVES: 225ft (69m), Very Severe (4c).
First Ascent: C. F. Kirkus, I. M. Waller, M. Pallis, May 1931.
Location: Right end of East Buttress, Scafell, Wasdale.

The route of Mickledore Grooves, on Scafell's East Buttress.

EAST BUTTRESS (RIGHT SIDE) — SCAFELL

MICKLEDORE GROOVES

O belay point

Mickledore Grooves—Summary

Just past and to the left of the big fault rift of Mickledore Chimney, near the right end of the crag, there is a clean, steep, sweeping slab. The climb starts left of this slab, below a rightward-sloping gangway.

1. 85ft (26m), (4c). Pull up the steep barrier wall to gain the gangway. Follow this rightwards to the bottom of twin grooves. Climb the left groove for 15ft (5m), then step into the right-hand groove with difficulty. Climb this to the belay ledge and large block belay on the edge of the steep sweeping slab.

2. 140ft (43m), (4c). Move right onto the slab and move up left to a diagonal crack. This leads rightwards through a bulge in the middle of the slab, and on to the corner groove on the right. Climb this to a ledge on the right. Traverse the ledge rightwards until a short, awkward wall leads to the top.

Mickledore Grooves—Description

As the eye scans the barrel-shaped East Buttress from Mickledore the first most attractive feature observed is the steep sweeping slab forming the left wall of Mickledore Chimney. The chimney was climbed as long ago as 1869 but the slab waited another sixty-two years before it was tackled. Mickledore Grooves enters from the side to climb the upper half of the slab. It was the first climb to tackle the steep, chiefly overhanging, walls of the East Buttress and its ascent opened up a new and formidable playground for the rock climber. It was a tremendous pioneering effort producing a flowing natural line. The leader of this bold route was Colin Kirkus— foremost Welsh rock climbing pioneer of the day.

This route must serve as one of the best introductions to the East Buttress. It is easily located and the line of the route is obvious giving continually interesting climbing in an increasingly impressive position. You start the route over to the left of the slab itself and immediately the overhanging nature of the East Buttress is apparent. The angle of the initial wall may prove somewhat of a surprise to the unwary. After this a ramp is followed right to the bottom of two steep grooves. By the time you reach the stance on the edge of the great slab you are beginning to get the feel of rock hereabouts.

The next pitch is both long and bold. It looks most unclimbable, with the consequence of failure, a fall down the sweeping rocks below, quite mesmerising. Today, with modern equipment, it is easier to relax and enjoy it, but in Colin Kirkus's day it must have taken a great deal of confidence and ability to launch off into this precarious world of steepness. Kirkus was said to be the master of delicate slab climbing and I don't think anyone experiencing Mickledore Grooves for the first time would argue with that. Fortunately the overlapping barrier in the centre of the slab, the position of maximum grip, reveals positive holds. Even so, when the slab is running water or damp and slippery it presents quite a challenge and these conditions go some way towards levelling the advantages of modern equipment.

The entry from the left is a natural one following the line of a steep ramp to gain the edge of the sweeping wall. In fact the direct ascent of the slab from bottom to top had to wait many years before it was ascended. Firstly, in 1936, the dynamic R. V. M. Barry struck a diagonal line across the slab to reach the original line some way after the start of the second pitch. Then in 1958 the brilliant Robin Smith forced Chartreuse (E1) but even then he was moved onto the left edge. Pete Botterill, with modern micro-runners, finally tackled it directly in 1979 to produce Midnight Express (E3) forty-eight years after the ascent of Mickledore Grooves.

This says something for the formidable steepness of the slab below the top pitch of the route. Not a place one would care to venture into protectionless in the 1930s. In fact one of the early ascents almost came to grief when Wilfred Noyce, belayed by Menlove Edwards, fell from the slab to end up in Mickledore Chimney far below. Incredibly cuts and bruises where his only injuries. When the slab is wet and greasy, so often the case because the cracks weep and the sunshine scarely reaches this most easterly-facing section of the East Buttress, one is extremely grateful for the frequent modern nut runners. The thought of falling without their protection is a nightmare too awful even to contemplate.

Mickledore Grooves is a full Very Severe and the undercut steepness of the East Buttress is apparent from the off. As interesting as the first pitch is, it is the solution to the sheer blank slab on the second that proves to be the most significant. Even with modern runners the situation is impressive and the climbing demanding enough to command

respect. One wonders what it was like in the early days. Was there grass growing here, similar to the grass caterpillars so much an early feature of the West Buttress of Clogwyn Du'r Arddu? If so, with the cracks choked, the climbing must have been formidable.

When it is dry, preferably on a warm summer's evening, the solid nature of the compact rock, the sureness and frequency of the holds, the excellence of the position on this bulging crag, make it a pure joy to climb. On such an occasion it is possible to savour the difficulties of the East Buttress, whilst still appreciating the boldness of its pioneers, without being intimidated—completely!

Gaining the ramp on the first pitch of Mickledore Grooves.

EAST BUTTRESS: Lost Horizons and Great Eastern by Yellow Slab

LOST HORIZONS: 245ft (75m), E4 (6b/a).
First Ascent: P. Livesey, J. Lawrence, September 1976. Free R. H. Berzins, M. Browell, 2 June 1981.
GREAT EASTERN BY THE YELLOW SLAB: 245ft (75m), Hard Very Severe (4c).

Lost Horizons and Great Eastern by the Yellow Slab on Scafell's East Buttress.

First Ascent: M. Linnell, S. H. Cross, 21 August 1931. The Yellow Slab, M. Linnell, H. Pearson, 10 September 1933.
Location: Central section of the East Buttress, Scafell.

EAST BUTTRESS (LEFT SIDE) — SCAFELL

The Yellow Slab

GREAT EASTERN BY THE YELLOW SLAB

LOST HORIZONS

belay point

Lost Horizons—Summary

Follow down the rake beneath the crag until the crag turns distinctly away. Above this is the central nose of the buttress and on its right a distinct clean cut and overhanging corner groove. This unmistakable and impressive line is the feature of the route. Start 20ft (6m) right of the lowest point of the crag.

1. 70ft (21m), (4b). Up the slab and short wall to swing left to gain a further slab leading to nut belays beneath the largest corner groove.

2. 125ft (38m), (6a/b). Climb the corner (peg runnner in place on the right wall) to a ledge and continue to near the top of the open groove. Originally there was a peg very high in the narrowing groove above and it was logical to first clip into this and then move left into a thin crack by undercutting the arete (6b). The peg has now gone and it is better and easier (6a) to step left from the groove, onto the arete across the wall below the crack. From a precarious position on the edge a move and a long reach enable the thin crack to be reached. This is climbed to an awkward small ledge. Step up the wall from its right end (hidden holds) then step right back into the groove (small wires in groove). Continue strenuously until the climbing eases. Climb up the groove, more in balance, up to the second and largest ramp crossing the groove. Belay on blocks beneath the crack splitting the headwall.

3. 50ft (15m), (5c). Climb the crack, which proves to be steeper and harder than it looks. A fitting end to the route.

Great Eastern by the Yellow Slab—Summary

From the same point as Lost Horizons beneath the central section of the crag, 20ft (6m) right of the lowest point scramble up and left to an overhung ledge.

1. 70ft (21m), (4b). Ascend the corner gangway passing a bulge at 20ft (6m) to layback into a crack and continue to an awkward sloping slab. Cross the slab to a

corner, move up until it is possible to pull out left onto the wall and climb to a good stance.

2. 110ft (33m), (4c). Step off the pedestal on the left to gain a steep crack which leads onto the end of the Yellow Slab. Ascend the slab to reach a steep wide crack at its top by a step left. Follow this to a shelf and belay.

3. 60ft (18m), (4c). Traverse left along the ledge until it is possible to move steeply up into a corner. Move left across the wall until some final awkward moves lead up to the top.

Lost Horizons—Description

This is one of the hard routes of the East Buttress which in no way compromises by traversing around or weaving through the difficulties. Direct from bottom to top it takes them head on, giving one of the purest lines on Scafell. For reasons not too difficult to comprehend, it escaped everyone's attention until Pete Livesey took up the challenge in 1974. The ethically minded criticised the mode of ascent. The runners were (it is reported) placed by abseil and a point of aid was observed from below. But the route is now all free—just within the E4 category.

It is not hard to interpret the inspiration for this route's name when belayed beneath the great open corner that constitutes its crux pitch. It really does overhang fiercely. The open sky observable from the rake disappears and the upward view reveals only rock. That tent of blue is only resighted after some very hard and particularly fine climbing.

Added to its grossly overhanging nature and the presence of ball-bearing like grey lichen the rock is tight and compact, generating the feeling that better holds would be offered if the whole crag were turned upside down. Consequently it is difficult to settle down and feel at home on the East Buttress. There just isn't time to adapt to the rock angle and undercut environment—immediately you start climbing it is strenuous and full weight. Lost Horizons does its best, however, and being a corner it allows you to break the grade somewhat by bridging out onto the walls. The holds and the runners are positive, which also helps, and you will soon have the bit between your teeth.

What a pity it has to go and get hard near the top of the groove. I have given it split grades here because there is a choice of direction. The original version clipped a very high peg runner in the top narrows of the groove then stepped left to finger holds in a thin crack. The move was effected by pinching, undercutting and laying off the blunt

At the bottom of the big corner on Lost Horizons.

arete. Hard—6b. This peg has now gone and it is logical, easier but still no push-over to move left across the wall a little way below the finger crack to the edge—6a.

It seems like a silly idea when you first arrive on the left edge of the groove. A few seconds will be spent wondering just how to maintain the status quo. But when you settle down you realise you are almost in balance and that it is only a short way from the finger crack. A technical move and a long reach bring it into reach and a further few feet of very steep ascent take you to an awkward ledge and a resting position.

You are now above the prominent groove which concentrates your attention from below. As you shake out, attempting to relieve

Starting up the bulging ramp of Great Eastern by the Yellow Slab.

some commitment. All good things must come to an end however and it is not long before the groove slackens in angle, crosses weaknesses and arrives at a comforting ramp and large block belays.

The crevassed block you bind yourself to is so big it must be safe—mustn't it? Anyhow the slight wall above with the generous crack in it looks easy; a pleasant contrast to the overhanging horror pitch below. You pull in, across left—and the sky disappears again.

Great Eastern by the Yellow Slab—Description

This is possibly one of the most pleasant and satisfying climbs of the grade in the Lake District. On inspection from the opposite flanks of Scafell Pike it is found to be a delectable line, winding its way through some very steep ground indeed; a ramp, a crack, a superbly beautiful light yellow slab appearing like an island of calm in a troubled sea, a wide smooth jamming crack, a traverse to a final overhang-capped corner, but with the possibility of a clean wall offering a chance to reach the horizontal above. If such rock features were to appear as lines of poetry the poem so composed could surely rival Wordsworth's 'Ode to Intimations of Immortality' as one of the finest in the English language. Whilst at the bottom of the Hard Very Severe category in terms of technical difficulty it is a long and sustained route taking a tentative weakness up the highest section of this most impending crag.

Although the very daring Maurice Linnell may be most noted for his pioneering exploits in Wales he actually hailed from Kendal on the doorstep of the Lake District. There he promised a local cobbler he would take his son climbing. Young Sid Cross found Maurice, motorbike and sidecar waiting for him after his rugby match one Saturday afternoon—the time had arrived. They headed for Scafell, bivouacked under a blanket on Mickledore and, after a dawn start, put up the Great Eastern. Their exploits didn't end there. They also went on to climb a number of routes on Scafell Crag—but that is another story.

A year passed before Linnell was to return to add the Yellow Slab finish to the route. It is a climb which from the start, up the leftward sloping ramp, takes you into sensationally exposed ground creating the distinct impression that you are burning your boats. But, as the first ascensionists discovered, those that dare, win—the impeccable rock of the Yellow Slab is a most worthy prize.

some of the pressure in your tired arms on the cramped and restricted ledge it begins to dawn that, even with the big groove below you, there is still an equal distance of rock above to complete this mega pitch.

Moves from the ledge are not obvious but runners in the groove on its right counter the swelling tide of uncertainty, despite the fact they are small and can only be placed after

WASDALE—SCAFELL CRAG

SCAFELL CRAG: Botterill's Slab, Moss Ghyll Grooves.
Map Ref: NY 208068.
Guidebooks: *Rock Climbing in the Lake District* by Birkett, Cram, Eilbeck and Roper. *Scafell, Dow & Eskdale* (FRCC Guide) by Al Phizacklea.
Attitude: Although the crag basically faces north the two routes here actually face west and get the afternoon sunshine.
Altitude: 2,700ft (820m).
Rock: Rhyolite.
Access: The quickest, most direct, approach is from Wasdale. From the car park at the head of the lake, near the campsite, a well defined track leads up by Lingmell Beck until a steep rib is reached. This is known as Brown Tongue and is followed into the recess of Hollow Stones (often used as a rock climbing base camp). Ascend again to pass a large boulder to the combe. Up on the right is the impressive expanse of Scafell Crag. The scree shoot on the right can be taken or a more direct approach made to the horizontal path along the foot of the crag (1. 5 hours).
Descent: The most usual is that of Broad Stand which is a well marked path leading down leftwards to Mickledore. At the bottom there are some short rock steps—negotiating these is

Moderate in difficulty. The spur of Mickledore is reached, not at its crest but a little way down its Eskdale flank—through a rock cleft behind a large detached boulder. Gain the crest and descend down a narrow scree gully to gain the horizontal path below the crag. The higher line above this is known as Rake's Progress and this leads directly under the start of Botterill's Slab.

Alternatively once on top traverse right across the plateau to the wide open gully of Deep Ghyll. This is descended until a path, West Wall Traverse, breaks off left (looking out) to avoid the chockstone below. This joins the distinct rift of Lord's Rake which leads down to the horizontal path below the crag.

Observations: Scafell Crag lies to the right of Mickledore, on the Wasdale side. Scafell is big and stretches in a long semi-circle. Despite its complexities the two routes selected here are immediately distinguishable from below. Botterill's Slab is the white clean slab set at right angles to the main face on the left side and Moss Ghyll is the huge widening chimney rift up the centre of the crag. Both Botterill's and Moss Ghyll Grooves face west, despite the otherwise northerly aspect of the crag, and they get the afternoon and evening sunshine. The rock, the situation and the climbing are superb.

The great face of Scafell Crag.

44

SCAFELL CRAG: Botterill's Slab and Moss Ghyll Grooves

BOTTERILL'S SLAB: 330ft (100m), Very Severe (4c).
First Ascent: F. Botterill, H. Williamson, J. E. Grant, 2 June 1903.
Location: Left side of Scafell Crag.
MOSS GHYLL GROOVES: 260ft (80m), Hard Severe.
First Ascent: H. M. Kelly, Blanche Eden-Smith, J. B. Kilshaw, 1 July 1926.
Location: Moss Ghyll is the central feature of the crag and this climb follows the interlinking grooves on its left wall.

Botterill's Slab—Summary

Start from the ramp named Rake's Progress directly below the slab.

1. 50ft (15m), (4b). Take the short chimney and continue to a belay beneath the slab.

2. 120ft (37m), (4c). Climb the slab by it's left edge. Pass a small ledge—the Crow's Nest—until thin cracks lead to the large ledge at the top of the slab.

3. 160ft (49m), (4a). Balance up the rib to gain the steep short chimney on the right. This is followed into the wide amphitheatre where the left rib provides the most interesting way to the top.

Moss Ghyll Grooves—Summary

Scramble up Moss Ghyll, avoiding the deep chimney by moving out onto the right wall, until an attractive groove cleaves up the left wall.

1. 55ft (17m). Follow the groove and over a block to belay in the corner.

2. 65ft (20m). Up the corner for a few feet until it is possible to transfer delicately across to the left edge of the slab. Follow the rib to a small ledge (possible belay). Continue up to gain the narrowing slab and at the top traverse across right to a ledge beneath another groove. This stance is known as the Look Out.

3. 80ft (24m). Climb the slab to a large ledge and recess.

4. 60ft (18m). Take the left wall of the gully to a rock ledge on the left. Step out onto this and then follow a vague line roughly in the centre of the wall (quite awkward to start) to the summit ledges.

Botterill's Slab and Moss Ghyll Grooves—Description

From below or opposite, on Scafell Pike or Lingmell, the great rock walls of Scafell Crag present an impressive sight. Walking into the combe beneath their feet is akin to entering a rare and precious sanctuary—the spiritual home of Lakeland rock climbing. There is plenty of choice here, and the range of difficulty is virtually complete. The two routes I have chosen are particularly special. Not only do they take two of the most appealing and distinguished lines up the cliff but the climbing, move for move, is continuously absorbing. Both offer tremendous excitement whilst their historical significance and excell-

Botterills Slab and Moss Ghyll Grooves on Scafell Crag.

SCAFELL CRAG

MOSS GHYLL

MOSS GHYLL GROOVES

BOTTERILL'S SLAB

belay point

ence of position provide the colourful icing to the cake.

The narrow white slab on the left of Scafell Crag is named after its first ascenionist; Botterill's Slab is a line that was just made to be climbed. Airy, technically difficult and virtually unprotectable (even with modern gear), its first ascent in 1903 was one of the most outstanding leads in the history of rock climbing. All who enjoy its delights today inevitably declare it a fantastic lead for that early stage of rock climbing.

'"How is it now?" my companions enquired, "Excellent," I replied, "a good belaying pin and just room for three. Do you feel like following?"' [1]

So wrote Fred Botterill in his account of the first ascent. He had completed 120ft (37m) of hard and unprotected climbing in fine style and without undue trouble. It was a brilliant achievement; an on-site lead without prior inspection. Feet clad in nailed boots, he held a full length ice-axe in one hand, sported a little rucksack on his back and trilby hat on his head. The ice axe was carried to remove loose rock and vegetation but he was to find precious little of either on the steep rocks above.

Typical of the man, Fred Botterill's account is a masterpiece of understatement:

'Traversing about 12 ft. outwards to the edge formed by one side of the crack and the face of the crags, I saw that with care we could advance some distance up this nose. Clearing away the moss from little cracks here and there I managed to climb slowly upwards for about 60 ft. The holds then dwindled to little more than finger-end cracks. I looked about me and saw, some 12 ft. higher, a little nest about a foot square covered with dried grass. Eight feet higher still was another nest and a traverse leading back to where the crack opened into a respectable chimney. If I could only reach hold of that first nest what remained would be comparatively easy. It seemed to be a more difficult thing than I had ever done but I was anxious to tackle it. Not wishing to part with the axe I seized it between my teeth and with my fingers in the best available cracks I advanced. I cannot tell with certainty how many holds there were; but I distinctly remember that when within 2 ft. of the nest I had a good hold with my right hand on the face, and so ventured with the left to tear away the dried grass on the nest . . . However, the grass removed from the ledge, a nice little resting place was exposed— painfully small, but level and quite safe. I scrambled onto it, but on account of the weight of the rope behind me, it was only with great care and some difficulty that I was able to turn round. At last I

Looking down to the final delicate moves of Botterill's Slab; a tremendously exciting position.

Moss Ghyll Grooves: beginning the short traverse right to the Look Out Stance.

out and that my companions had already attached a further 60 ft. Further, I began to wonder what had become of my axe, and concluded that I must unthinkingly have placed it somewhere lower down. There it was, stuck in a little crack about 5 ft. below me. I succeeded in balancing it on my boot, but in bringing it up it slipped and clattering on the rocks for a few feet took a final leap and stuck point downwards in Rake's Progress. Standing up again I recommenced the ascent and climbed on to the second nest à cheval, from where, after a brief rest, I began the traverse back into the crack. This was sensational but perfectly safe. As usual I started with the wrong foot, and after taking two steps was obliged to go back. The next time I started with the left foot, then came the right, again the left, and lastly a long stride with the right brought me into the chimney. The performance was what might have been called a pas-de-quatre.'

Scarcely mentioned because of the magnitude of that 120-ft slab is the interest to be found in the next section. However directly you attack it—and if the rib is followed without deviation it is tricky—you arrive in an awkwardly sized chimney rift. This proves interesting even in its present clinically clean condition. In Botterill's time it was crammed with loose chockstones . . . 'and debris formed a roof' which must have added yet another dimension to his already monumental efforts of the day. Above this you can amble easily to the top in a number of localities but the rocks on the left offer the most attractive route.

A few months after Botterill's marvellous ascent there was a tragic accident on the Scafell Pinnacle. Four climbers roped and climbing together, as was customary in those early days, were attempting a climb pioneered by O. G. Jones when the lead climber fell. He pulled off the next man and so on until all four climbers fell to their deaths. It had a sobering effect and brought home the fact that Fred Botterill's ascent was a phenomenal effort, something quite out of the ordinary. A cross, which is there to this day, was carved on the rocks beneath the foot of Scafell Pinnacle and it was to be many years before climbers returned with earnest intent.

Despite the fact that Moss Ghyll Grooves doesn't quite make the Very Severe rating it is a very modern-looking line. The shallow scalloped grooves rising up the face to the right of the centremost part of the Central Buttress are placed most dramatically to scale the full height of the crag. Slim and elegant, if they had been just a few degrees steeper they would have been substantially more difficult.

H. M. Kelly was a modern thinker in many

could sit down on the nest and look around me.

'The view was glorious. I could see Scafell Pike and a party round the cairn. Far below was another group intent on watching our movements, a lady being amongst the party. I once read in a book on etiquette that a gentleman in whatever situation of life should never forget his manners towards the other sex, so I raised my hat, though I wondered if the author ever dreamed of a situation like mine. I now discovered that our 80ft. of rope had quite run

EAST
BUTTRESS

MAIN FACE

PISGAH
BUTTRESS

PINNACLE

DEEP
GHYLL

BROAD STAND
(Descent)

RAKES
PROGRESS

MICKLEDORE

WEST WALL
TRAVERSE
(Descent)

STEEP
GHYLL

LORD'S
RAKE

PATH

MOSS
GHYLL

A view of the whole of the Wasdale
face of Scafell seen from Pike's crag.

ways and his bold imaginative climbs reflect that fact. He worked on the apparently formidable line of Moss Ghyll Grooves over a number of years, top roping and gardening it in sections, until he finally realised its feasibility and fitted it all together in one glorious push.

It is all interesting, best climbed in the afternoon sunshine, and the nut runner protecting the extremely delicate crux moves, moving left onto the edge on the second pitch, will not be shunned by many. Following the sensationally exposed rib above is one of the most delectable climbs to be experienced—on any route, on any crag. Above the interest does not wane until the summit rocks are reached.

On a clear day, above this mountain crag, the view can be just as breathtaking as the climbing. The one-time landlord of the Wasdale Head Inn (then known as the Huntsman's Head Inn), the fabled auld Will Ritson, summed up the situation in his own unique way. He declared, to a Bishop he had just guided to the summit, that there were seven kingdoms in sight:

'Yonders the Mull of Galloway, the Kingdom of Scotland—one; then, west are the Mourne Mountains, the Kingdom of Ireland—two; then south is Snowdon, the Kingdom of Wales—three; off St. Bees Head is the Isle of Man, a kingdom of its own—four. The top you are standing on is the Kingdom of England—that's five. . . . Don't ye, a priest, preach that the Kingdom of Heaven is above, and that of Hell deep below us? There's six and seven for ye.'[2]

It's often hard to leave Scafell Crag on a summer's evening as you always feel that there is time for another route. For it is at the end of the day, as the sun sinks west, that the crags are the most effectively lit with its golden light. And why should you? Let the valley blacken and the lights twinkle, leave the world to go about its business. Enjoy the quiet of this special place.

After a full day on the rocks of Scafell, perhaps capturing the early morning sunshine on the East Buttress, moving onto the Scafell crags in the afternoon, and then climbing Mickledore Grooves, Moss Ghyll Grooves and Botterill's Slab, as the sky reddens and the shadows begin to gather you may find there is no call to venture higher to discover Auld Will's sixth Kingdom. However, should the wind blow cold or the rain begin to fall, the desire to go deep below may become overwelming—and tomorrow's another day to climb on Scafell.

1. 1903 *Yorkshire Ramblers Club Journal*—'Two New Climbs on Scafell' by Fred Botterill. 1903.
2. *Fell & Rock Climbing Club Journal*—'Stories of Auld Will Ritson' by W. T. Palmer.

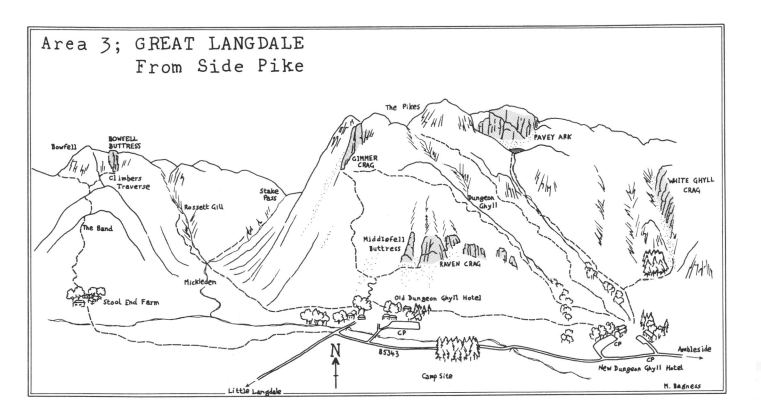

Area 3; GREAT LANGDALE
From Side Pike

M. Bagness

GREAT LANGDALE—BOWFELL BUTTRESS

BOWFELL BUTTRESS: Bowfell Buttress.
Map Ref: NY 245069.
Guidebooks: *Rock Climbing in the Lake District* by Birkett, Cram, Eilbeck and Roper. *Great Langdale* (FRCC Guide) by M. G. Mortimer.
Attitude: Faces east.
Altitude: 2,250ft (680m).
Rock: Rhyolite.
Access: It is best to park at the Old Dungeon Ghyll and from here follow the road (to right angled bend) and then the track to Wall End Farm. Continue up the Band towards Bowfell. As the spur levels out and before the final pull up to the Three Tarns below Bowfell itself take the path leading off steeply up to the right. This soon levels off into an undulating traverse which leads to a large scree shoot. This is crossed to gain the foot of Bowfell Buttress (2 hours). This is known as the Climber's Traverse and crosses underneath Flat Crags to arrive beneath the great slab on the right of which stands Cambridge Crag and then the scree shoot down the gully to the left of the Buttress. Returning to the Old Dungeon Ghyll from the foot of the Buttress, it is probably best to descend directly to Mickleden—the valley floor—below.
Descent: From the top of the Buttress descend to the left to gain the large scree shoot.
Observations: This is a high mountain crag and the time and energy expended to reach the climbs should not be underestimated.

BOWFELL BUTTRESS: Bowfell Buttress

BOWFELL BUTTRESS: 350ft (107m), Very Difficult.
First Ascent: T. Shaw, G. H. Craig, G. R. West, C. Hargreaves, L. J. Oppenheimer, 24 May 1902.
Location: Bowfell Buttress, Bowfell, Great Langdale.

Bowfell Buttress—Summary

Start just left of the foot of the Buttress.

1. 75ft (23m). Take the line of weakness up the rocks to the left of an obvious corner situated some 40ft (12m) up. Cross to gain the corner and climb the short chimney on the right. Continue to a terrace.

2. 100ft (30m). Take the easy wall above then move diagonally left to a sentry box in the chimney. Climb the chimney and continue over ledges to gain a large terrace sloping down to the right. Move down right for 25ft (8m) to a crack in the steep wall.

3. 55ft (17m). Climb the 15ft (5m) crack which is surprisingly difficult and insecure to pull out onto slabby rocks. Move across left

and up to a ledge and large pinnacle belay (the Gendarme).

4. 60ft (18m). Move left into a groove and ascend this to a chimney. This can be tackled directly or, slightly easier and more usual, on the wall on the right until steepening rock forces a long stride back left into the corner. Move up until a large platform on the left provides stance and belay.

5. 60ft (18m). Step back right and up until a groove can be followed off to the left. This leads to the top. Alternatively, and harder, the rocks on the right can be followed in an exposed position.

Bowfell Buttress—Description

Great Langdale has long been a major focal point for rock climbers. The goings on at the Stool End and Wall End Barns are as much a part of climbing folklore as are the doings of an earlier generation at Wasdale Head. Whilst things are a bit more formal and organised

Looking up Great Langdale with Bowfell on the left and the Pikes on the right.

these days there is still ample accommodation to suit a wide variety of tastes. Most importantly the rock and the climbs are just as enjoyable as they ever were and there is tremendous choice. Whether it be a Moderate on the rambling walls of Pavey Ark or an E6 up the beetling central face of Raven Crag above the Old Dungeon Ghyll, here is the rock for climbing.

Whilst I may be accused of bias, understandably as Little Langdale is my home town and the crags of Langdale my formative stamping ground, I put it to you that many of the climbs to be found hereabouts are amongst the best in Lakeland.

A moderately long mountain route that takes some beating, is a climb named simply—Bowfell Buttress. No need for anything longer, or cleverer, or even offensive to capture the attention. One can see the buttress hanging below the summit of Bowfell from the Old Dungeon Ghyll a few thousand feet and a couple of miles away. The route climbs the front of this. Once climbed the name won't be forgotten.

The approach, which is a long way by English standards, should be enjoyed as an integral part of the climbing day. The Band, often a mass of struggling humanity, is a slog. It's best just to switch off and get on with it—only pausing to pay due homage to the magnificent conical rocks of Gimmer across the Langdale valley over to your right. In due course the branch off to the right leads steeply onto the shoulder of Bowfell.

Take heart because as the edge is crested a hidden, gently undulating path leads scenically and easily across to the very foot of the buttress. This is the Climber's Traverse. It first passes underneath the strangely structured and appropriately named Flat Crags. Here the banded, light coloured and undercut rhyolite lies horizontally and more resembles a sea cliff than a high mountain crag. At its end, a boon on a hot day, there is a fine mountain spring issuing water directly from a fissure in the rock.

Above is the great slab, a huge sweeping rock shelf that provides an interesting way up to and down from the summit of the moun-

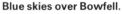
Blue skies over Bowfell.

tain. But across the large scree shoot lies the buttress itself. A grand bastion of rock, it appears to be formed with an infinite layer of vertical ribs—the flat bands of Flat Crags taken and turned from the horizontal to the vertical. It is a crag structured purposely for the rock climber.

It reclines back from the vertical just enough to give one a chance. Just a few degrees steeper and the Bowfell Buttress would be quite a different proposition. As it is, it is consistently entertaining—difficult enough to be interesting without being desperate. Full weight exposure is always there too and towards the top its heavy presence will not go unnoticed.

Quite remarkably for a mountain crag of this size and altitude, all the climbing is on excellent rock, with little or no grass or moss to interfere with the perfect unity of boot and rock. This and the positive nature of the holds, despite the high gloss achieved at the height of the season, make it a sound choice of climb for wet conditions. The stances are comfortably generous, with sound belays, and coupled with this the large scale of the face makes it suitable for large parties. Thus attacked, when the clouds roll over the summit of Bowfell, it will provide an enjoyable and demanding outing.

Bowfell Buttress is one of those routes that logically unwinds as you progress, and despite being the easiest progression, it holds much interest. The starting rocks lead to an awkward chimney, which in turn leads out onto the buttress front. This polished chimney must have witnessed many a struggle but—very much a case of initiation by fire—it is the vital key that unlocks the entrance to the front of the buttress.

The sentry box at the start of the straight chimney is a useful place to rest and gain composure. Then it's rapidly up to the large sloping shelf and down to the insignificant-looking crack in the wall above. This is only short, and whilst the wall looks steep the crack looks a bit of a giveaway.

Its not. This is the technical crux and proves to be both strenuous and precarious. Numerous parties have come to grief here whilst frantically scrabbling for something more positive on the sloping slabs above. There isn't a lot and if it wasn't for the fact that it's short and there's a substantial ledge below to mask the drop temporarily, this section could have upped the overall grading of the route quite significantly.

There is quite a noticeable feeling of com-

Bowfell Buttress.

mitment after this section is passed. The moves across the sloping rocks to the substantial pinnacle belay known as the Gendarme are usually taken with a certain stoic steadiness by the leader. A little time lashed on here and perhaps a chocolate bar to replenish nervous energy will restore the enthusiasm. But it still requires a significant degree of commitment to actually get underway again.

A crack gives a superb nut placement. Specifically a Friend 2 goes in remarkably well but it is one of those cracks which so easily accepts but can be reluctant to release—take

On the sloping holds at the top of the crux wall of Bowfell Buttress.

care not to bottom a Friend so placed. A problematical corner chimney is reached and proves very awkward. Steeper rocks to the right will be found to have better holds but even so there comes a time when one is forced to make a long, balancey step back left into the corner. Almost immediately above, a large ledge brings respite and another oppor-

tunity to savour the position.

Another 60ft (18m) of rock climbing takes you to the top. Imagine climbing that for the first time. What would you name it if you did? 'A Long Exposed Mountain Route On Perfect Rock With Continually Sustained Climbing And Some Really Interesting Bits'?

No—Bowfell Buttress says it all.

Looking across to the North-West Face of Gimmer Crag.

GREAT LANGDALE—GIMMER CRAG

GIMMER CRAG: Ash Tree Slabs/'D' Route (Combination), Gimmer Crack, Gimmer String.
Map Ref: NY 277069.
Guidebooks: *Rock Climbing in the Lake District* by Birkett, Cram, Eilbeck and Roper. *Great Langdale* (FRCC Guide) by M. G. Mortimer.
Attitude: Faces north-west.
Altitude: 1,600ft (490m).
Rock: Perfect rhyolite.

Ash Tree Slabs, Gimmer String and Gimmer Crack on the North-West Face.

Access: From either the New or Old Dungeon Ghyll Hotels.
New: Take the path leftwards to cross the Dungeon Ghyll and follow the steeply rising, zig-zagging path until it levels off. Continue until, just after it starts to take to the steep fellside again, a small path branches off left. This leads to the south-east face of Gimmer (1 hour).
Old: Take the steep path leading up through a small re-plantation scheme until it is possible to exit from its left-hand top corner to gain steep scree. Trudge up this to find a well defined narrow path which eventually leads to the south-east face of the crag. Alternatively ascend Middlefell Buttress (see RAVEN CRAG) and continue directly up the hillside above to intercept the level path that originates from the New Dungeon Ghyll Hotel (1 hour).

On reaching the face drop down to the toe of the rocks then climb steeply back up the other side until North West Gully is reached (15 minutes).

Descent: Into North Gully via Junipall Gully—an awkward, steep descent, or to the south-east face via South-East Gully—easier but still steep. Gimmer Crag forms a head separated from the steep hillside by these two obvious gullies, which both start at the same point. South-East Gully can be entered from a lower point so dispensing with a few feet of scrambling above the climbs. Finding this point is not easy, the gully walls are vertical elsewhere, so if in doubt continue up and back to the source of the gullies.

Observations: The reddish-grey rock of Gimmer is outstandingly clean, hard and compact. This and its position, perched on steep ground yet effectively sheltered by the hillside behind, make it into one of Lakeland's finest climbing crags. It dries quickly and the north-west face takes the afternoon and evening sunshine.

GIMMER GRAG
NORTH WEST FACE

Crux overlap

Forked Lightning Crack

THE BOWER

'D' ROUTE

Pedestal

Ash Tree Ledge

GIMMER CRACK

Base of routes obscured by this ridge

belay point

ASH TREE SLABS

GIMMER CRAG: Ash Tree Slabs/'D' Route (Combination)

ASH TREE SLABS: 160ft (49m), Very Difficult.
First Ascent: G. S. Bower, A. W. Wakefield, 20 June 1921.
'D' ROUTE: 120ft (37m), Severe.
First Ascent: G. S. Bower, P. R. Masson, 18 April 1919.
Location: North-west spur and west face, Gimmer Crag, Great Langdale.

Ash Tree Slabs—Summary

Just before the path levels and reaches North-West Gully there is a corner with a fine slab springing from it.

1. 50ft (15m). From the base of the corner move up and left across the slab to reach the edge. Climb it to a rock ledge on the left.

2. 110ft (34m). Climb to the ledge above and on into the groove. Continue up directly to belay on Ash Tree Ledge.

'D' Route—Summary

Takes the obvious steep cracks up the West Wall directly above Ash Tree Slabs. Scramble up to a narrow long ledge below the triangular recess which marks the start of the steep cracks.

1. 120ft (37m). Take the groove to gain the recess. Traverse left for 15ft (5m) to the fault and follow it back right to a ledge and large block (possible belay). Climb the Forked Lightning Crack into a sloping corner just below the top. Climb the corner crack to finish. Belays further back.

Ash Tree Slabs/'D' Route (Combination) —Description

The combination of these two routes provides a very satisfying and logical line up the sunny side of Gimmer. The climbing is remarkably consistent, the balance climbing experienced on Ash Tree Slabs contrasting markedly with the steeper wall of 'D' Route above.

Gimmer, seen from the road at the head of the Great Langdale valley is quite distinctive. Even from this distance its shape and colour, that of a reddened rectangular obelisk stood on end and split down the centre, plucks at the rock climber's heart strings. The image is no less inspiring as you draw near to its foot. But this is its south-east face. Around the other side, placed secretively out of sight, lies something even better.

The whole topography of Gimmer could be likened to the rump of an elephant. Viewed from below or opposite we see that the red-grey hard-skinned animal is a powerful beast. The west face, sitting high above a vegetated heel, is smooth and rounded but her north-west flank rearing larger and longer with the folds and wrinkles of slabs, cracks and overhangs begins and ends independently. It is a 200ft (61m) wall created solely to entertain the rock climber.

To get from one side to the other you must drop down and circumnavigate the heel. When you do, and join North-West Gully after first descending beneath the south-east face and then slogging back up the steep hillside, the effort involved will be amply rewarded. The rock for climbing here is quite magnificent and its variety outstanding.

Although best combined to reach the top of Gimmer, both the routes described here have their own special qualities. Ash Tree Slab provides delectable climbing with considerable exposure. In effect it is an angle cut from a more continuous and steeper wall and as you move left onto the edge you get the opportunity to observe the full force of the severity below. 'D' Route looks much harder than it actually is. It was a bold lead up the headwall of the west face in 1919 taking the distinctive crack subsequently named the Forked Lightning Crack. Although originally graded Very Severe the excellence of the holds now available place it squarely in the Severe bracket.

Grit expert George Bower climbed 'D' Route first and at that time this formed the most left-hand and hardest of the Gimmer alphabet climbs. It was a fitting culmination to the initial pioneering exploits on the west face. (Another generation was to pass before the ascent of 'F' Route—see *Classic Rock Climbs In Great Britain* (Oxford Illustrated Press)—by Jim Birkett and Vince Veevers heralded another era of difficulty.) Surprisingly Bower left the ascent of Ash Tree Slabs for two further years. But significantly his exploration at last took him round the elephant's heel to initiate the development of the incredible north-west face.

After completing this superb slab he immediately realised that linking this and 'D' Route provided a tremendous way to reach the summit of Gimmer. The first FRCC Red

Gaining the crack on 'D' Route.

The spectacular profile of the North-West Face of Gimmer. The climber in red is on 'D' Route, with the second belayed on Ash Tree Ledge below.

Guidebook commented thus:

'The author of this climb and the D crack suggests a combination of the two; covering as they do, practically the whole length of the Western face, they prove a full course of soup, fish, meat, and "afters", with a cigarette or pipe on the balcony at the finish.'[1]

This guide to Langdale also records that two ash trees marked the start of the climb—they are long since gone and the whole corner is now whistle clean and of open aspect. Immediately you start from the small bay at its foot the climbing is interesting. The holds, typical of much of the climbing on Gimmer, are never very large but even when distinctly small they provide a positive grip for hand or foot. The traverse across to the edge is interesting and the climbing remains of about the same technical difficulty all the way. But as you reach the edge of the slab and continue up the rib the climbing becomes wonderfully exposed.

The large terrace of Ash Tree Ledge provides a comfortable place to linger and many parties take a picnic at this point. And why not? If bad weather threatens or for any other reason you should wish to get down then it is possible to descend by striking an arc over to the right. If the correct line is chosen scrambling leads down to the Luncheon Ledge—the point of arrival at the south-east face.

Above the Forked Lightning Crack can be seen to rent the wall, offering a possible way up the otherwise smooth final hundred feet. Climbers viewed from afar, from the terraced ridges opposite or from the summit of Pike O' Stickle, really give the impression of being fly-like on the wall. The position is Very Severe, the climbing always absorbing and varied, but the technicalities never exceed the Severe category. There are a number of belaying possibilities but to lead it in one long aesthetic run-out will bring out its best qualities. However, remember to extend any runners placed because the direction and nature of the pitch is such that quite considerable drag will ensue if you don't.

1. 1927 Guidebook Published by the Fell and Rock Climbing Club—*Great Langdale and Buttermere* by George Basterfield.

GIMMER CRAG: Gimmer Crack and Gimmer String

GIMMER CRACK: 240ft (73m), Very Severe (4b).
First Ascent: A. B. Reynolds, G. G. Macphee, 5 May 1928.
GIMMER STRING: 250ft (76m), E1 (5b).
First Ascent: J. A. Austin, E. Metcalf, D. Miller, 15 July 1963.
Location: North-west face, Gimmer Crag, Great Langdale.

Gimmer Crack—Summary

Soon after the path scrambles up North-West Gully there is a prominent crack emanating from the corner on the right. Start beneath this.

1. 85ft (26m), (4b). Enter the steepening corner crack and climb it until it is suitable to move delicately left out across the wall. A groove is gained and followed to a ledge and large pinnacle block belay.

2. 85ft (26m), (4b). From the top of the pinnacle step onto the wall and using the thin cracks effect a mantleshelf move into the horizontal break. Move across, up and left to a rock ledge. Climb the steep rib, a long reach being a distinct advantage, until a traverse leads back right into the corner crack. A few feet of awkward ascent lead to the naked rock ledge—the Bower.

3. 70ft (21m), (4c). Continue directly up the crack to the small overhang. It is arguably best to face right to make height to surmount it. Keep in the corner crack, passing a ledge, all the way to the top.

Gimmer String—Summary

Start as for Gimmer Crack.

1. 110ft (33m), (4b). Follow the first pitch of the crack to the base of the pinnacle block then move across right to a larger block in the corner beneath a wide crack.

2. 60ft (18m), (5a). From the top of the blocks move right into the base of a wide chimney crack. Follow this to a stance in the corner groove above. (This groove is followed by Kipling Groove.)

3. 80ft (24m), (5b). Move up the groove until a traverse can be made to gain the niche in the arete. The shallow groove above this is followed until it is easier to move left around the arete. Move up on good holds until the wall steepens. This is taken directly, utilising a thin crack, until a step right enables a move up to be made to a ledge and then the top of the crag.

Gimmer Crack and Gimmer String—Description

Known historically as The Crack the distinctive corner rift up the north-west face of Gimmer was one of the most remarkable first ascents of the 1920s. George Bower was the first to examine its possibilities and was lowered from the top down to a distinctive ledge beneath the topmost and steepest section. He was top-roped out and reported that the difficulties were considerable. His exposed starting point for the ascent was the strategically positioned rock ledge now appropriately named the Bower.

Facing page, top:
Tackling the crux on Gimmer Crack.

Facing page, bottom:
The crux section of Gimmer String, starting the moves right.

The awkward section leading to the Bower on Gimmer Crack.

58

'His opinion of "The Crack" was not such as to encourage future explorers, or raise any hopes of ultimate success.'[1]

The deed was reported thus in the 1927 Great Langdale Guide:

'This crack is about 120 feet in length, vertical, rope-climbed, but still unled.'[2]

The bait so blatantly laid proved irresistible and the following season's guidebook saw the first lead of this imposing problem in its entirety:

'Now, a remark like that almost amounts to a throwing-down of the gauntlet, and probably many people have wondered if this crack would be climbed. From much talking, a reputation for supposed inaccessibility was built up which earned for it the simple but distinctive name of "The Crack". . . . In April, 1928, A. B. Reynolds, out for blood, definitely aspired to its conquest. Having encountered a kindred spirit in the shape of H. G. Knight, a start was made on the 21st April, 1928. the reason for this direct assault, without a preliminary trial on a rope held from above (a permissible precaution, in view of the reputed difficulty of the climb!), appears to be a chance remark that surely nobody would do such a thing. This shows the danger of saying anything that could possibly be construed into a challenge, implied or otherwise.'[2]

It was a remarkable effort and the team succeeded in reaching the Bower. There they stuck—unable to negotiate the overhang in the crack above. A rope lowered from the top effected a rescue though not before 'they admired the sun-set over Rossett Ghyll and saw the moon appear'. But with appetite whetted Reynolds returned a week later with the veritable G. G. Macphee to lead the Crack clean from top to bottom.

In fact the Crack is a much more interesting climb than the name would suggest. At least a third of the route takes the steep open wall to the left of the corner, ensuring that a wide range of climbing technique must be utilised to achieve success.

After the initial corner begins to rear uncontrollably an escape across the left wall is made. This in itself is both technical and delicate requiring a positive commitment. Already the calibre of that 1920s ascent makes itself felt.

The next section, stepping from the exposed top of the pinnacle block, is again a remarkably committing exercise, but even this is exceeded by the very next move: a forced mantleshelf into the horizontal weakness.

Above this a rock ledge and then steep rib requiring a ridiculously long reach leads to an easy horizontal traverse back into the corner.

The moves up to gain the famous Bower ledge are nothing less than brutal. The corner crack expands to chimney-like proportions only to close again to offer nothing but a thin crack to assist progress in reaching the Bower. A degree of skill is required to maintain the position of legs and body in the chimney void as the hands search out the possibilities for holds on the blankness above. In fact during the first ascent a precariously jammed flake provided a valuable aid to progress but this fell out on the third ascent! It was noted that it bounced only once before exploding in the gully below.

This ledge forms a solid spring-board from which to tackle the final, and most demanding, section of the crack. Impressively placed and considerably exposed, it hangs on the vertical right wall of the corner with a straight drop to North-West Gully, an uninterrupted 150ft (45m) below. In the early days, although providing a convenient place to rest, there was no belay to be had. Only the advent of nut runners have made it a haven from which to belay a struggling second or leader both in comfort and safety.

I remember my father giving me quite specific advice on just how he climbed the crux section of the corner crack above. 'When you get to the steep bit—you'll know it when you get there—just face right and use the square cut holds on the edge. Like little dominoes they're small but quite positive. An amazing lead for the 20s.' But whatever method you employ to make height at the overlap, some 40ft (12m) up the final corner, there is still a long reach to be made to find the hold in the crack above. Thankfully it is a tremendously generous jug enabling a secure launch to be made over the bulge into the easier crack above. Plain sailing remains now to the top.

Despite the passage of time this route loses none of its honest virtue. Fashions may come and go but this thoroughly solid climb will entertain and thrill the climber ad infinitum. And perhaps when the rocks are a little greasy, as is often the case on the crux, and the wind blows a little chill, an ascent will be found to be no run of the mill affair. But if inclement conditions do prevail and thought of using aid does cross the troubled mind then remember the words of G. G. Macphee:

'It must be understood that in this expedition no

artificial aids were used—a practice becoming deplorably prevalent even in our homeland climbs. No loops of rope were previously placed at strategic points for use as handholds, stirrups, or possibly worse. Not a step was cut, not a piton was driven in, not even an artificial chockstone was inserted in "The Crack." '[1]

Gimmer String occupies a tremendous position up the steep and airy arete to the right of the Crack. Viewed equally from above or from below the final section gives the appearance of being desperate. Allan Austin was the leader responsible for stringing it all together, a bold effort in 1963, and it is now one of the pleasantest routes of the grade on Gimmer.

The north-west face of Gimmer has always been one of my favourite evening crags. If you are determined, the ascent from the valley car parks can be made in less than half the time indicated in the information given here, depending on how keen and how fit you are. In the heady height of summer we often used to leave Kendal, some fifteen miles away, after finishing work at 6 pm, to climb on these sun-kissed rocks. On such an occasion, if you are climbing confidently, Gimmer String is a very good choice of route.

The initial pitch is really that of the Crack. Then unless you are of such a size that you actually get jammed in the chimney there should be no problems to slow down the momentum. The next section is where the real interest begins and it is immediately steep from leaving the security of the corner of Kipling Groove.

A niche hanging in the arete leads to a technically absorbing groove. Near the top of this, as it becomes increasingly hard, there is a blind move out left onto the wall. The hidden jug used, if you can find it, is magnificent but the position gained by the swing left is incredibly exposed. Good holds lead to the final intimidating headwall. This is the bit that looks desperate. It is the crux but I won't say any more, you must work it out for yourself— Allan Austin had to!

Enjoy a summer evening climb on Gimmer; perhaps as burning hot recedes into quiet cool, when the sensation of heat through finger from rock brings unseen pleasure. Or should the falling sun be enveloped by cloud and the rain begin to spot, then savour the newly liberated sweet smell of freshly damp rock, when the brittle crispness of dried lichen suddenly sponges to softness beneath the touch. And should the thunder crash and lightning lick the sky and the heavens open, and should your pulse quicken only to recede

as the storm quietens into steamy heat, then enjoy all these experiences to be found on a summer's evening on Gimmer—the climber's crag.

1. 1928 *Journal of the Fell & Rock Climbing Club*—'The Crack' by G. Graham Macphee.
2. 1927 Guidebook published by the Fell & Rock Climbing Club—*Great Langdale and Buttermere* by George Basterfield.

Martin Bagness making the traverse left across the wall on the first pitch of Gimmer Crack.

GREAT LANGDALE—RAVEN CRAG

Raven Crags stretch across the fellside. Middlefell Buttress on the far left and Far Far East Raven on the right.

RAVEN CRAG: Middlefell Buttress, Pluto.
Map Ref: NY 285065.
Guidebooks: *Rock Climbing in the Lake District* by Birkett, Cram, Eilbeck and Roper. *Great Langdale* (FRCC Guide) by M. C. Mortimer.
Attitude: Faces south and is quick to dry.
Altitude: 650ft (200m).
Rock: Rhyolite.
Access: From the Old Dungeon Ghyll car park (15 minutes).
Descent: From Middlefell Butttress enter and follow the gully down to its left. From Pluto move over to the right a short distance until the path scrambles down onto a pinnacle block and then a terrace behind an oak tree. This leads easily across and down. Alternatively it is possible to traverse left and descend awkward rocks into the gully on the left of the buttress—but this is slippery if wet and not recommended.

Observations: The attractions of Raven Crag are many—not least its accessibility and nearness to the Old Dungeon Ghyll! A little care should be taken with the rock in places but generally both the rock and the climbing are of good quality.

RAVEN CRAG: Middlefell Buttress and Pluto

MIDDLEFELL BUTTRESS: 250ft (76m), Difficult.
First Ascent: J. Laycock, S. W. Herford, A. R. Thomson, 24 September 1911.
PLUTO: 225ft (69m), Hard Very Severe (5a).
First Ascent: A. L. Atkinson, 1958 (Pitch 1), P. Woods 1953 (Pitch 2), E. Metcalf, J. Ramsden, 1957 (Pitch 3).
Location: Raven Crag, Great Langdale.
Map Ref: NY 285065.
Guidebooks: *Rock Climbing in the Lake District* by Birkett, Cram, Eilbeck and Roper. *Great Langdale* (FRCC Guide) by M. C. Mortimer.
Attitude: Faces south and is quick to dry.
Altitude: 650ft (200m).
Rock: Rhyolite.
Access: From the Old Dungeon Ghyll car park (15 minutes).
Descent: From Middlefell Butttress enter and follow the gully down to its left. From Pluto move over to the right a short distance until the path scrambles down onto a pinnacle block and then a terrace behind an oak tree. This leads easily across and down. Alternatively it is possible to traverse left and descend awkward rocks into the gully on the left of the buttress—

but this is particularly slippery if at all wet and is not recommended.

Middlefell Buttress—Summary

This is the detached buttress to the left of the main crag. There are at least three possible starts, all from the same area directly below the toe of the buttress and all leading to the same point.

1. 50ft (15m). The easiest start, and possibly the most entertaining, takes the rift on the left. Squeeze through this and continue to ascend behind a large pinnacle to a platform then a larger ledge. Right of this, the central start, is a polished crack guarded by a short steep wall. This is the problem start and is highly glossed and far from easy. Right again is a shallow groove which again proves interesting. Take your pick!

2. 150ft (46m). A wall behind the ledge leads to a ledge. Moves left lead to a ledge with a short chimney groove on the right. Climb into this and continue up more or less

Middlefell Buttress and Pluto on Raven Crag.

directly until a large terrace is reached with an embedded boulder of some size.

3. 50ft (15m). Walk across to the next wall above, the Curtain Wall. Start from the right and ascend diagonally leftwards into the centre of the wall. A steep pull over an overlap leads to easier climbing and the fellside above.

Pluto—Summary

Starts below the centre of the crag by scrambling up to below the clean-cut corner crack.

1. 50ft (15m), (4c). Climb the crack directly, exiting right near the top and continue to belay on the large pinnacle on the terrace.

2. 90ft (27m), (5a). Step onto the wall and traverse rightwards until direct ascent up a small groove leads to the large overhangs. Continue right below the curving roof until a blind step down leads to the crossing of a scruffy groove. Belay on the terrace on the right.

3. 85ft (26m), (5a). Move back left and climb the rib of the groove until a steep move up and right leads onto the face of the wall

(crux). Climb straight up, over an overlap, to gain a traverse line. Move left to gain a groove and continue directly until a step left leads to a scrambling finish and belay—a little way back.

Middlefell Buttress and Pluto—Description

Middlefell Buttress takes the separate buttress above the farm of the same name. Traditionally it was climbed as a means of approach to Gimmer Crag. Whilst it remains the most direct and pleasant way to Gimmer it is also a popular and highly worthwhile route in its own right. Its large stances, excellent views and fairly non-serious nature make it a good route for all seasons.

The first ascent team included S. W. Herford of Central Buttress fame (see *Classic Rock Climbs in Great Britain*) and it would be no surprise if they climbed the problem start—up the steep polished central crack. Those of you who try this may be quite surprised as to its difficulty. It involves some precarious moves on what is now highly slippery rock. More than one experienced

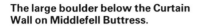
The large boulder below the Curtain Wall on Middlefell Buttress.

Above:
Hard moves from the rib lead
rightwards onto the final Steep Wall
of Pluto.

Left:
The Curtain Wall on Middlefell
Buttress.

leader has come to grief here, falling a few feet from the bottom of the crack to ignominiously twist an ankle or break a leg.

Care too should be exercised on the final wall—the Curtain Wall. Although not hard it must be treated with due respect. A simple traverse in from the right (or from the left if you wish) suddenly lands you on steep ground and although the holds are good they must first be found before a strenuous pull can be made. After the pull it isn't over and concentration should not be allowed to wane.

But I am looking at detail, and this you will discover for yourself, so I will return to making some general points that should be appreciated. Combined with the simplicity with which the line can be varied to suit climbing ability, the large ledges and easy escape available into the gully on the left make it a suitable route for the inexperienced. The position of the Old Dungeon Ghyll, immediately below, may allow the chance to strike and return quickly even on the most inhospitable of days. And apart from the convenience of it, it is a route of some considerable character commanding fine

views of the head of the Great Langdale valley.

Pluto is one of those inexplicable anachronisms. The route doesn't so much follow a line as link three independent pitches. It starts on one side of the crag and finishes on another. Yet for some reason the thing works. The climbing is good, surprisingly good, and once underway the direction seems totally logical.

Climbing historian, ex-president of the Climber's Club *et al*, Trevor Jones was buzzing his way through the Lakes when we met. Keen to hit rock, but with only a limited time schedule, I suggested we try Pluto.

'Pluto hmm—never heard of it,' he said, seeming a little sceptical that a mere HVS on little Raven Crag should be suggested. 'We'll give it a go Trevor—perfect route for the day,' I said. 'O.K. Bill—you're the Lakes expert.'

I'm sure he was totally unconvinced right until he focussed on the steep clean corner crack that marks the start. 'HVS Bill, looks harder.'

'No it's only VS, the start, Trevor.'

'Surely not, looks hard, I'll give it a go.'

Once underway I observed that Trevor's

Squeezing through the cave start of Middlefell Buttress.

climbing technique much resembled his quick-fire, staccato, conversation. 'Good holds, tremendous, what a surprise only VS,' and he was up. 'Belay over on the big detached pinnacle Trevor,' I shouted as the rope snaked out.

'Incredible, what a position, looks hard.' Trevor crossed the wall on the second pitch and seemed to dive up for the roof some 15ft (5m) up. 'Watch the rock Trevor, it's a bit shattered,' I cautioned. 'Look up the wall—that's Centrefold—straight up.'

'Looks steep, where now.'

'Put in a runner Trevor, then traverse right to the end, drop down—it's a blind move but keep the hands low and just step down—there's a good foothold and the moves across the gully are easy.'

'No holds, oh, right I'm going across.'

He was there—the rope was snaking yet again. Despite the number of times I've done this traverse it always surprises me just how steep and exposed the wall is to reach the overhangs. Then just how shattered are the flakes and blocks you put your gear around. And just how gripping is the final step down when the traverse shelf ends. Trevor had placed a nut just above the move and all seconds in this position, with nothing until the belay some 25ft (8m) horizontally right, will appreciate a thoughtful leader.

'Where now Bill?'

'Go left onto the edge, then straight up to a high hold and pull around onto the front face.'

'Looks steep, not much here.'

'No there isn't a lot really Trevor.'

'Oh, looks hard.'

A high reach, above a not overly protected rib reveals enough to justify you launching out, which Trevor did to good effect into the middle of the steep finishing wall. 'Looks hard, steep, where now?'

'Straight up Trevor, there's a horizontal break where you can rest and get a good runner, then straight up again to a traverse line that leads easily left.'

'Looks hard, sustained, right.'

Up and up and on to the top. 'Good route quite hard, that final wall, sustained, what grade?'

'Well done Trevor, good lead, 5a.'

'5a!'

'Lakes 5a Trevor.'

GREAT LANGDALE—PAVEY ARK

PAVEY ARK: Arcturus/Golden Slipper (Combination), Astra.
Map Ref: NY 286080.
Guidebooks: *Rock Climbing in the Lake District* by Birkett, Cram, Eilbeck and Roper. *Great Langdale* (FRCC Guide) by M. C. Mortimer.
Attitude: Generally faces south but Astra on the gully wall faces east.
Altitude: 1,700ft (520m).
Rock: Rhyolite (vegetated below Jack's Rake—better above).
Access: From the New Dungeon Ghyll go directly up to Stickle Tarn. The crag is probably best approached by walking round the left side of the tarn (45 minutes).
Descent: From Golden Slipper go left and down to find the top of Jack's Rake—the large diagonal break crossing the crag. From the top

of Astra go over to the right and descend down East Gully.
Observations: Despite its rather vegetated and generally motley appearance Pavey Ark offers some very good climbing. It is a lot bigger than first appearances would suggest and the insignificant-looking walls and buttresses, dwarfed by the whole picture, are found to be quite substantial when one begins to climb. The gully on the right is East Gully and its main wall offers much hard climbing. The diagonal break is Jack's Rake. Both provide an easy way up or down the crag. Beware of stonefall particularly when climbing on the walls below Jack's Rake. Although the crag tends to weep for a long period in certain areas on the whole the sunny disposition dries the rock reasonably quickly.

An aerial shot looking down onto Stickle Tarn nestling below the cliffs of Pavey Ark.

Arcturus, Golden Slipper and Astra on Pavey Ark.

PAVEY ARK: Arcturus/Golden Slipper (Combination)

ARCTURUS: 270ft (82m), Hard Very Severe (5a).
First Ascent: J. A. Austin, E. Metcalf (var), 28 April 1963.
GOLDEN SLIPPER: 200ft (61m), Hard Very Severe (5a).
First Ascent: J. A. Austin, R. B. Evans, 19 July 1958.
Location: Pavey Ark, Great Langdale.

Arcturus—Summary

Traversing across from the foot of Jack's Rake the climb lies on the first continuous wall which is joined by the path. Directly 100ft (30m) above there is a prominent hanging prow of rock (taken by Cruel Sister E2). A short slab skirts the base of the vertical wall above—there is a dirty gully/groove on the right and a small holly above the slab. Start beneath this.

1. 120ft (37m), (5a). Up the slab and move left to the holly. Climb the steep barrier until a ledge gives a good handhold. There is sometimes a peg runner above this but if moves are made to stand on the ledge then step back down and traverse to the left at a low level. This way gives the easiest access onto the slab. Climb the slab and bear left to a good ledge below a steep corner break in the overhangs.

2. 150ft (32m), (4c). Move right and climb the corner. Cracks then lead directly up the wall to a ledge and nut runner. Traverse right beneath the overlap and cross the exposed and delicate slab to make a step down to ledge and belay.

3. 50ft (15m), (4c). Move right to gain a very steep rib and climb this until easier ground leads to Jack's Rake.

To reach Golden Slipper follow up Jack's Rake passing the deep and narrow rift of Gwynne's Chimney.

Golden Slipper—Summary

There is a slim pillar of rock some distance up. Start about 60ft (18m) left of Gwynne's Chimney where a short wall guards a slight rightward-sloping weakness.

1. 60ft (18m), (4c). Climb the wall following the gangway right to a ledge. Moves lead directly up the ledge below the pillar.

2. 80ft (24m), (5a). Climb the front face of the pillar directly to gain and follow a slight groove. At the top of this move right to ascend directly to a large ledge at the top of the pillar.

3. 60ft (18m), (4a). Follow the rib on the left until easy ground leads up to the top.

Arcturus/Golden Slipper (Combination) —Description

It has to be said that the rock below Jack's Rake does not look particulary inspiring to climb on. But before you seek compensation for the steep approach and plunge into Stickle Tarn try Arcturus. This combined with Golden Slipper gives ample reward for the effort of getting to Pavey—then you can take that swim feeling satisfied with your day's work.

After the easy initial section there is a steep impenetrable-looking barrier guarding the slabby wall. Arcturus solves the problem quite ingeniously by finding a line of quite reasonable holds. Because you are reaching high, on slightly impending ground, it is not easy to see exactly what you are pulling on. But the holds feel big enough, if somewhat rattly, and lead to a recessed ledge. It provides a good handhold and the route, at the 5a grade, goes left at this level to gain the slabby wall above the barrier further over, though many people pull into the recess and stand in it. Usually there is an old peg that can be clipped reaching from here, but some make the mistake of pulling straight up the wall to gain the slabby rocks above and left. Whilst this can be done it is nearer 5c than 5a and the route at the HVS grade actually moves, inconspicuously, left at a lower level.

If the low line is taken the climbing remains at a reasonable standard and satisfactory holds will be found to pull up onto the slab. Lovely positive finger-holds now, at an angle where most of the weight can be taken on the toes, lead on up the wall to ledges below the next steep section. The real scale of this previously insignificant-looking wall is now becoming revealingly apparent.

Good steep climbing, on tremendous holds, leads to a delicate slab below an overlap. The exposure here is quite something and the

On the edge nearing the top of the pillar of Golden Slipper.

moves right feel quite awkward and precarious. A good nut can be placed before the slab and one, not so good or obvious, at its right end before a teetering step down brings you to the belay ledge.

The next section, the final pitch leading to Jack's Rake, is a lot more interesting than first appearances suggest; a short rib but surprisingly steep with not a great deal between it and the scree now some 200ft (61m) below. A walk over to the left leads to the start of a

High on the pillar of Golden Slipper.

really tremendous piece of climbing. It may be best to coil the ropes, despite the fact the journey is only a short one, because there is a lot of loose rock and scree on the rake and the consequences of dislodging anything onto any climbers below would be disastrous.

The route takes the clean-looking pillar high up—best viewed before you get right underneath the start. In the afternoon sun the rock reflects a golden glow and it looks magnificent. The first pitch is only a means to reach the pillar. You take the front of it.

The rough, pocketed rock is absolutley superb. Pavey Ark is noted for the roughness of its rhyolite above the fault line of Jack's Rake and this is the best of it. Just the right side of vertical with little to nothing in the way of protection, this is an immaculate piece of climbing; always in balance, always interesting, delicate and exposed with the hardest

boldest section at the top, where the gear is most spaced. A superb equation of challenge and reward.

The big ledge provides a host of bilberries, Pavey Ark's speciality, with a tremendous view across Stickle Tarn down the Langdale valley to Lake Windermere and on and on. Now the world seems to have almost stopped, indeed for a time on the pillar below there was only you and the rock in front of your face. Time now to reflect on a quite incredible piece of balance climbing, technically mild for the grade but interesting enough to ensure you remember the importance of each finger pocket.

Nothing could really follow that but even so the rib is very pleasant. Scrambling leads to the top and if the sun's still strong and the air warm don't forget the swim—it's an almost compulsory end to the perfect day.

ASTRA: 300ft (91m), E2 (5b).
First Ascent: J. A. Austin, E. Metcalf (alt), D. G. Roberts, 27 May 1960.
Location: East Gully Wall, Pavey Ark, Great Langdale.

Astra—Summary

About halfway up the gully the unmistakable twisting pillar of Astra stands above the lower mossy slabs. Start directly below the nose where, from a small subsidiary gully, entrance onto the mossy slabs can be made.

1. 100ft (30m), (4a). Move onto the slab and move up trending leftwards to a grassy terrace. Traverse across left to climb the short steep wall into a groove and up to a good ledge in the corner just left of the pillar.

2. 70ft (21m), (5b). Move right across the base of the wall to the arete. Runner in thin crack. Move round and ascend diagonally rightwards to a good flake on the steep nose. Runner on the flake and good nut up above the flake and slightly to its right (not easy to see). Move up and left to gain a slab and continue up this to gain a little corner in the face of the pillar. Step up the wall and pull right round onto the edge (hidden pocket for the hands on the edge). There is a stance, on the front of the pillar, immediately above.

3. 130ft (40m), (5a). Continue up the narrowing slab above to the base of a V-groove. Climb it (hard if wet) to a large ledge. Finish up the short crack above this. Scrambling then leads to the top.

Astra—Description

The East Gully Wall is terrain for the Extreme climber. Its key sections are chiefly overhanging and the rock has a far from generous nature. Despite the development of a mass of hard routes, many of them of excellent quality, one route stands out, for my money, above the rest of the pack. That route, one of the earliest to be climbed here, is called Astra.

The line is not super-direct, indeed there are variations which straighten it out—with a considerable increase in difficulty—but it flows naturally, weaving along the line of least resistance up the imposing twisted pillar. The nature of the climbing is such that it is simultaneously strenuous and balancey. The holds, whilst being positive and even sharp in places, are generally always small and the front of the pillar is categorically vertical—and even steeper below.

It is best to get onto it when the sun illuminates the face in the morning, cold fingers are definitely unwelcome on a climb of this nature. It all really begins on the second pitch. A few moves from the stance brings the arete to hand. Transferring round from here

The route of Astra on Pavey Ark.

EAST GULLY WALL
PAVEY ARK

Flake

relay point

ASTRA (Bottom section obscured)

Above:
The thin moves right to the flake on the edge of the pillar.

Above right:
A rest and some security can be found on the flake.

onto the front face, from safe in-balance to strenuous commitment is psychologically if not physically the hardest section. Reaching the security of the large flake on the edge of even steeper ground only 15ft (5m) away is by no means an automatic procedure. But a rest can be taken here and there is a runner, a really excellent nut up and slightly right of the top of the flake.

It's still steep as you launch off again but the angle soon relents when a slab on the left is gained. Now the nature of the climbing changes. The runners are sparse, non-existent before micro-wires, and a cool controlled approach is required to work out the continuing technicalities up and then back right, to find again the rearing steepness of the pillar's front.

There is a little square-cut groove here and some thin cracks. On the first ascent a peg was placed and used to move through the verticality. It was almost twenty years old when a

Scotsman flew from above and pulled it—he landed in the gully at the foot of the pillar without touching rock in between. Somehow he survived to tell the tale. Today a reasonable nut protects the next few crux moves.

If you know just how to do it, reaching the right level and pulling round onto the rib, it isn't actually the crux. Working it out is very satisfying and the belay ledge arrives immediately after the moves are made.

Above the climbing may be a lot easier but it is equally magnificent. Roughened grooves and narrowing slabs pull you up into the blue sky. Then there is a ledge and a V-chimney which can actually prove desperate if things are wet and greasy. A bit more, then the top.

All the fine routes selected here are the work of Allan Austin. I once asked Allan what was his favourite climb of the many he pioneered in the Lakes. He admitted to the fact that he was 'glowing with pride' after the ascent of Astra. Who wouldn't be.

GREAT LANGDALE—WHITE GHYLL

Looking up to White Ghyll with the upper crag lit by the sun.

Opposite:
The crux of Astra seen from across East Gully.

WHITE GHYLL: Haste Not, Haste Not Direct, White Ghyll Wall
Map Ref: NY 298071.
Guidebooks: *Rock Climbing in the Lake District* by Birkett, Cram, Eilbeck and Roper. *Great Langdale* (FRCC Guide) by M. C. Mortimer.
Attitude: Faces west.
Altitude: 1,500ft (460m).
Rock: Rhyolite.
Access: From the New Dungeon Ghyll Hotel, Stickle Barn (large car park at the side or smaller car park at the edge of the road opposite hotel entrance) where White Ghyll can be seen as a nick in the skyline up to the right, follow the path and immediately on leaving the hotel cross a little bridge over on the right. Continue along this path through a gate to gain a wide open track. Soon after this a kissing gate on the right opens to a narrow track leading along a stone wall. Follow along this, through the wood to the bottom of the Ghyll itself. Straight up the Ghyll to a lone tree (sycamore) situated beneath the first set of crags—Lower White Ghyll. Continue

to a convenient boulder situated beneath the large bands of overhangs that constitutes the Upper Crag (30 minutes).
Descent: Either go up and across left to gain the head of a scree gully which drops to the base of the crag or go down right where a track drops down and then up again (do not mistakenly continue to descend down and left (looking out) because this drops over the crags of Lower White Ghyll) to an easy rake ending below the start of White Ghyll Wall. If the latter descent is taken, extreme care must be taken not to dislodge any loose rocks or scree as these fall directly over and into the popular climbing ground of Lower White Ghyll.
Observations: The steep right-hand wall of the gully (looking up) is naturally split, by the descent rake, into two climbing areas of great character—Upper and Lower White Ghyll. The larger of the two, Upper White Ghyll crag, consists of an impressive series of banded overhangs and all the routes here offer exciting climbing with plenty of exposure.

WHITE GHYLL: Haste Not, Haste Not Direct and White Ghyll Wall

HASTE NOT: 190ft (58m), Very Severe (4c).
First Ascent: J. Birkett, L. Muscroft, 9 May 1948.
HASTE NOT DIRECT: 185ft (56m), E2 (5c).
First Ascent: A. Austin, R. Valentine, 2 May 1971.
WHITE GHYLL WALL: 220ft (67m), Mild Very Severe (4b).
First Ascent: J. Birkett, L. Muscroft, T. Hill, 9 May 1946.
Location: Upper White Ghyll, Great Langdale.

Haste Not—Summary

On the left of the most overhanging section of the crag the rocks lean back—White Ghyll Slabs—and dividing the main crag from these slabs is a distinctive chimney (White Ghyll Chimney) with a ledge on its right-hand side about 50ft (15m) up. Haste Not starts beneath an inverted V-roof in an alcove about 35ft (11m) right of the bottom of the chimney.

1. 70ft (21m), (4b). Climb the short barrier wall to the corner beneath the inverted V-roof and step left across the wall to gain entry to the front of the buttress above. Continue directly to the large ledge (the chimney is immediately to the left) then traverse right to take a small stance, with good nut belays, on the rib.

2. 50ft (15m), (4c). Move up the wall and transfer steeply rightwards to move up into a position below the large overhangs. A gangway moves across rightwards. Follow this with an interesting move sliding backwards down the bottomless groove to gain the rib on the right. Pull up and swing around this to a ledge and belay by another groove (Gordian Knot).

3. 70ft (21m), (4b). Step left and pull through an awkward inverted V-bulge from where easier climbing leads to the top.

Haste Not Direct—Summary

Starts in the corner just right of Haste Not.

1. 60ft (18m), (5a). Climb the corner

Haste Not, Haste Not Direct and White Ghyll Wall on White Ghyll.

Phil Burke bridging the steep corner that starts the 2nd pitch of Haste Not Direct.

directly to the roof and move across right onto the rib. A belay can be taken here—adequate anchors but small stance—or it may be found preferable to descend to the ledge below on the right (belay stance of Gordian Knot).

2. 80ft (24m), (5c). Move left and up into the narrow groove, tape runner on the right wall. Pull out onto the slab on the left and continue steeply to the traverse of Haste Not. Rest and runners. Above is a bulging crack, pull into it and climb it until the wall above eases and a belay can be taken.

3. 45ft (14m). Pleasant rocks lead easily to the top of the crag.

White Ghyll Wall—Summary

Starts at the right side of the overhanging main crag. A rib, with a small tree in a cave up above it to the left, marks the start.

1. 80ft (24m). Start by the foot of the rib and follow it to a large ledge beneath the overhangs. Move across right to a block belay at the foot of the undercut corner groove.

2. 50ft (15m), (4b). Climb the corner scoop and up over the overlap to continue diagonally leftwards up the wall to gain a recess and belay (hidden from below).

3. 90ft (27m), (4b). Descend the groove to move delicately left across the ribs to gain the sweeping clean wall in an exposed position. (A more direct entry can be made onto the wall but it is harder and the climbing inferior.) Climb the slabby wall to the top.

Haste Not, Haste Not Direct and White Ghyll Wall—Description

As ghylls go White Ghyll is one of the most attractive. As crags go White Ghyll one of the fiercest. For the climber, preferably in the evening sunshine, there isn't anything else quite like it.

The red and white rocks of the stream bed are followed until the straight Corinthian-like corners of Lower White Ghyll first come into view. Some excellent routes but our destination lies, past the lone sycamore, further and higher up the ghyll. First impressions of this upper crag are correct, bands of overhangs culminate in a great, apparently impenetrable, final wave before merely vertical rocks lead gently to the grassy crest 150 vertical feet (45m) above.

The routes selected have markedly different characters. They all extract the best of the contrasting qualities to be found here. However they do have one thing in common—sensational exposure. On the right of the crag White Ghyll Wall meanders in from the side, finding a key to the smooth slabby wall above the great overhangs by a natural line that avoids major technical difficulty. Over to the left, passing through a V-roof entrance en route to the heart of the overhangs, lies Haste Not. Aptly named, it provides a rather ingenious way through the barrier of overhangs. Starting a few feet to its right, more or less centrally, the eliminate of Haste Not Direct strikes a direct link through the bulges. It is a route very much in the modern idiom.

The delightful slabs on the left and the narrow steep chimney were, naturally enough, the first bits of White Ghyll to be ascended. But the main face remained inviolate until 1940 when Jim Haggas and Miss E. Bull charged through the central overhangs (Gordian Knot). An extraordinary ascent for the day (Haggas only ever made three first ascents but they were all set in the same desperate mold) it was not until my father, Jim Birkett, repeated the climb some five years later that anyone else was to take on the challenge of this remarkable crag. He went on to record some ten routes here and those with vision quickly realised that the ghyll provided one of best and most demanding climbing crags in the Lakes. A roadside crag, outside the traditionalist's vocabulary, White Ghyll set the stage for a new wave of climbing attitude and difficulty.

It is the position adopted by Haste Not that makes it into a very special climb. Cunningly it threads its way, side-stepping a V-roof and up a clean wall, up to nudge the final most overhanging barrier. There is no way through here at anything easier than 5c and it was a brave effort to pull onto the steep guardian wall to spy the hidden ramp crossing rightwards. A magnificent link, hung in space, providing a safe passage through the hostilities to the comfortable possiblities beyond; but not one to be taken for granted—all those sliding down the knee-scraping finger-scrabbling bottomless groove will experience fluttering hearts before powerful jugs swing you safely through the exposure.

Haste Not Direct is in every sense an eliminate taking a very direct line from the right-angled corner at its bottom to the impressive bulging crack through the final overhanging barrier. Yet it is also a natural line connecting the slight weaknesses that penetrate through the overhanging barriers on this intimidating wall. Allan Austin finally put it all together as one route. He did not climb the final overhanging crack until some years

after he had claimed the rest below.

Even in its original form, which traversed off along the ramp of Haste Not, it provided a highly absorbing climb. I well remember my first attempts to quit the narrow groove that starts the second pitch, making those committing moves onto the steep wall to its left. My team, tucked safely below on the stance of Gordian Knott, resorted to the singing of hymns as I thoughtfully pondered my position. But once across things moved rapidly enough; there is little point in lingering on this steep and strenuous wall. Once committed there is little respite until the ramp of Haste Not is reached. Here there is rest and security. In those days you traversed off and it still seemed a good route.

On the next occasion the object was to complete the route including the direct finish up the crack. At that time I had been weightlifting as a means of keeping fit during the winter months. One of the exceptionally strong regulars had decided to try climbing. He had done some quite reasonable routes and reckoned they were easy, so I offered to take him out one evening. Climbing well, no doubt benefiting from the gym, the whole route including the direct finish up the crack didn't offer any problems. Indeed all I can

remember about the final bit was the weight-lifter swinging in space as I hauled him up the top crack.

I mentally recalled the incident as I photographed Phil Burke in the same position on the top crack. He didn't find it unduly easy (it was quite mossy at the time—his being probably the first ascent of that season) and so I have concluded that really big muscles aren't the main requirement here. Good old Lakes cunning must be the secret of success and holds will be found on the wall to the left of the crack. But it is a good route whatever—yet another Allan Austin creation employing his famous 'climbing craft'.

In many ways White Ghyll Wall is one of my favourite climbs. It provides slabby balance climbing that is technically quite reasonable. Yet you find yourself in the most superb of positions—out on a slabby wall of perfect rock with the most generous helping of exposure imaginable. It seems such an elegant thing to do, to toe tap in from the side, to reach the most delightful location on White Ghyll without having to heave and grunt through the overhangs directly below.

Out on the wall, in or out of the evening sunshine, is a distinguished place to be.

Above left:
Phil Burke committed on the final overhanging crack of Haste Not Direct.

Above centre:
Fred Snallam moving across to the infamous bottomless groove of Haste Not.

Above:
The magnificent final pitch of White Ghyll Wall.

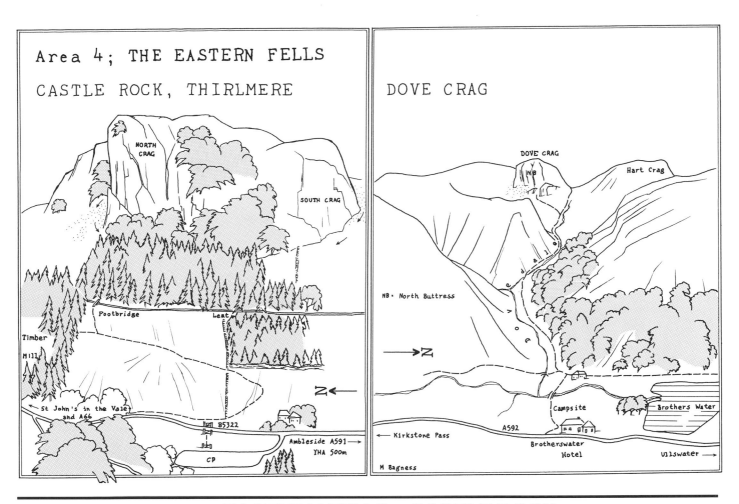

Area 4; THE EASTERN FELLS

CASTLE ROCK, THIRLMERE

NORTH CRAG

SOUTH CRAG

Footbridge

Leat

Timber Mill

St John's in the Vale and A66

B5322

CP

Ambleside A591→ YHA 500m

DOVE CRAG

DOVE CRAG

Hart Crag

NB = North Buttress

NB · North Buttress

Campsite

Brothers Water

A592

← Kirkstone Pass

Brotherswater Hotel

Ullswater →

M Bagness

EASTERN FELLS—CASTLE ROCK

CASTLE ROCK: Zigzag, Thirlmere Eliminate.
Map Ref: NY 322197.
Guidebooks: *Rock Climbing in the Lake District* by Birkett, Cram, Eilbeck and Roper. *Buttermere & Eastern Crags* (FRCC Guide) by J. Earl, A Griffiths and R. Smith.
Attitude: Faces west.
Altitude: 800ft (240m).
Rock: Volcanic (a volcanic plug) giving very good flake holds.
Access: Plainly visible from the Ambleside—Keswick road (A591) it is approached from the constructed car park on the St. John's-in-the-Vale road (B5322). A path leads from the centre of the car park across the road to a stile. Skirt round the hill first right, then aim for the top left of the field to reach a small wooden bridge crossing the aqueduct to gain the wood. Follow up to the large boulder beneath the crag (15

minutes).
Descent: Either down a steep gully to the left (moderate scrambling) or a circuitous journey round to the right, first over then beneath the south crag.
Observations: In many respects the ultimate roadside crag, Castle Rock guards the entrance to St. John's-in-the-Vale. The South Buttress lies to the right, on which there are a number of pleasant climbs of reasonable standard, with the striking sheer face of the North Buttress over to the left. The ascent of Overhanging Bastion (see *Classic Rock Climbs In Great Britain*— Oxford Illustrated Press) up the formidable-looking ramp in the centre of the north face was a particularly fine lead for its period but there are, in addition, very many superb climbs on this tremendous crag. Two such climbs are described here.

CASTLE ROCK: Zigzag and Thirlmere Eliminate

ZIGZAG: 305ft (93m), Very Severe (4b).
First Ascent: R. J. Birkett, C. R. Wilson, L. Muscroft, 22 April 1939.
THIRLMERE ELIMINATE: 185ft (56m), E1 (5b).
First Ascent: P. Ross, P. J. Greenwood (var), 26 June 1955.
Location: North Buttress of Castle Rock, Thirlmere, Eastern Fells.

Zigzag—Summary

On arrival there is a large rock where it is convenient to gear-up and leave the sacs. The route takes the diagonal ramp, from right to left, on the wall immediately above. Start by scrambling 30ft (9m) up to the tree at the foot of the ramp.

1. 95ft (29m), (4b). Follow the ramp to its end then ascend directly to a large ledge.

2. 50ft (15m). Traverse easily rightwards to a big flake or ash tree belay.

3. 80ft (24m), (4b). Move onto the clean smooth wedge slab above and move across right to steep cracks. Climb directly to belay in the corner on the large ledge.

4. 80ft (24m). Take the big slab on the left, traversing to its edge for maximum exposure.

Thirlmere Eliminate—Summary

Start about a rope length over to the right of the arrival stone. The rock here rises clean and unbroken by trees. (The first pitch is actually that of Rigor Mortis, also climbed by Paul Ross, because it gives a more consistent standard of climbing.)

1. 50ft (15m), (5a). Take the wall to a corner below a small overhang. Step out right and ascend directly to the belay tree on the large ledge.

2. 75ft (23m), (5a). Move across diagonally leftwards to gain the corner groove. Ascend this steeply until it is possible to pull out onto the left arete (tape runner). Follow this directly to a sloping ledge and take an awkward belay in the corner above (old peg).

3. 60ft (18m), (5b). The imposing corner above is climbed directly. There is a bulge at 15ft (5m) and pulling round this (reasonable runner below), up into the corner constitutes the crux. However, the difficulties above are sustained.

Zigzag and Thirlmere Eliminate—Description

An attractive and exciting place to climb Castle Rock is steep, high, and has a selection of climbs and grades to entertain most tastes. The best time to visit is afternoon and evenings, when the sun comes full on to warm the rocks. The two routes I have selected here are chosen for contrasting reasons.

Thirlmere Eliminate offers a good challenging climb, reaching full strength with its imposing top pitch. Zigzag is quite different. Nowhere could the climbing be described as dramatic, neither could the line be thought of

Castle Rock showing Zig Zag and Thirlmere Eliminate.

CASTLE ROCK

ZIGZAG
(First section obscured)

THIRLMERE ELIMINATE
(First section obscured)

○ belay point

Above:
Beginning the ramp behind the ash of Zig Zag.

Above right:
Chris Bonington tackles the crux surmounting the overlap to enter the steep final groove of Thirlmere Eliminate.

as powerful. Its inclusion is based on its being a thoroughly enjoyable climb in a good position, with enough interest for the many who would like to amble their way up this rock bastion without resorting to anything more desperate.

It was pure chance that Chris Bonington happened to be ascending Thirlmere Eliminate as I was photographing Zigzag. Never one to lose out on an opportunity I swung across from photographing Steph and John to capture Chris and his companion in action on the latter. It's during moments like this that you wish you could be in two places at once. Controlling one climbing team for the camera is difficult enough, two somewhat more so. But, thanks to a good degree of tolerance and co-operation from all concerned, the objective was achieved.

The ramp of Zigzag crosses a very steep wall, quickly assuming a position of some exposure. Then just as you are developing confidence and getting going, there is a cut through the ramp—a rather blank-looking gap when you most need the holds. Crossing this is technically the crux, requiring some concentration whatever your climbing form. The leader should remember to safeguard the second adequately here by placing a worthwhile runner *after* the gap—even though he may not need it to protect himself.

The next pitch, with great position but no difficulty at all, takes you rightwards across the face to find a little wedge slab just meant for climbing. Above this the crack is interesting, though it is now quite polished and can be particularly awkward when wet. Finally, although the last zag up the large sweep of finishing slab is also very easy, the rough rock makes it a pure delight to climb. To enjoy it to

Above left:
Looking up to the North Buttress of
Castle Rock.

Above centre:
Chris Bonington on the rib of the 2nd
pitch of Thirlmere Eliminate.

Above:
Stephanie Snowball on the crux of
Zig Zag where the rope disappears on
the 1st pitch.

the full aim for its left edge to soak up all the exposure of the entire North Buttress. Finishing on the top as the evening sun sets blood red behind distant friendly hills is the connoisseur's way to taste this rather pleasant wine.

Paul Ross and Pete Greenwood, both leaders of the highest calibre, are noted for their particularly tough and brutal first ascents up overhanging rock. Names like the Bludgeon and Hell's Groove immediately spring to mind. Theirs was a hard school and their climbs very much reflect the attitude—all or nothing. I think their outlook was best summed up one night for me by Pete who looked at me, fag in hand, over the pints of beer spread across the table in front of us and said: 'Who cares about the view?'

An absorbing climb with three excellent pitches Thirlmere Eliminate is a very natural line and one of the most satisfying on Castle. With modern gear much of the seriousness has been removed but that is not to say there are no exciting sections—it is still necessary to climb some good way above your protection.

I have described the first pitch of Rigor Mortis to take you directly to the tree belay— on the dry ledge. This I think gives a standard of difficulty consistent with the climbing on the next two pitches. The original pitch climbs just left of this, utilising a large flake. The way, as described, looks innocuous but many will be taken unawares by the angle of the wall as they swing up right out of the corner. Steep climbing on excellent holds, giving a good warm-up for what lies above.

The groove and hanging rib that follow give the most elegant positional climbing of the route. The exposure and paucity of nut runners whilst out on the arete make for measured movement and the delicate pull onto the sloping slab above requires a controlled approach. But there are good finger holds and, so typical of the climbing on Castle, the flake holds prove to be both frequent and excellent.

The final groove packs quite a punch and should not be underestimated. Laybacking around the bulge and gaining a bridging position in the groove is more than a little interesting. Above the climbing hardly relents until the trees are reached some 40ft (12m) higher. A good runner can be placed below the bulge but don't waste strength attempting to place something in above the bulge until you bridge up above it—whatever your sophisticated rack there is nothing worthwhile here. Good old-fashioned neck and the ability to go with it are the main requirements.

An absorbing climb—who needs the view!

Final Groove

Resting ledge

Crux traverse

O belay point

FEAR AND
FASCINATION

EASTERN FELLS—DOVE CRAG

Dove Crag showing Fear and
Fascination.

DOVE CRAG: Fear and Fascination
Map Ref: NY 376109.
Guidebooks: *Rock Climbing in the Lake District*
by Birkett, Cram, Eilbeck and Roper. *Eastern
Fells* (FRCC Guide) by J. Earl, A. Griffiths and R.
Smith.
Attitude: Faces north-east.
Altitude: 2, 000ft (610m).
Rock: Rhyolite.
Access: From the Brotherswater Hotel or
campsite car parks (permission required for
both) take the track across to Hartsop Hall.
Continue on the track until the right fork can be
taken. This leads up into Dovedale. After a
stream is crossed the crag can be observed over
to the left. The main track ascends to the right of
it and if this is taken it is necessary to traverse
horizontally left, over a shoulder, to gain the

bottom of the crag. Alternatively a more direct
approach can be made, taking a natural gully in
the front of the shoulder, to the foot of the crag
(1.25 hours).
Descent: From the end of the climb traverse
right to gain the well-worn descent path (this
path leads up to the large cave situated just
above the North Buttress).
Observations: Dove is a big crag, both in size
and impact. The route described here tackles
the North Buttress which lies on the right side.
The rock on the North Buttress is better than the
rest and is generally clean and sound offering
good incut holds. However, this piece of rock is
the most continually overhanging in the Lake
District and presents a superbly sustained
challenge.

DOVE CRAG: Fear and Fascination

FEAR AND FASCINATION: 175ft (53m), E5 (6a).
First Ascent: R. Graham, B. Birkett (shar), 26
June 1980.
Location: Dove Crag, North Buttress, Dovedale,
Patterdale, Eastern Fells.

Fear and Fascination—Summary

The North Buttress is the compact and grossly
overhanging wall on the right side of the crag.
Just before (to the left of) the large boulder
which abuts against the wall at its centre there
is a flake crack leading to a rock ledge.

   1. 25ft (8m), (5a). Climb the flake crack to
belay on the ledge.

   2. 150ft (46m), (6a). From the right end of
the ledge pull over the bulge passing an old
peg and continue up the wall to a flake block.
Climb straight up for 10ft (3m), runner in
pocket to the left, to reach the rightwards
traverse line. Move across this (technical
crux) to gain a groove and step up to a less
strenuous position and old peg/bolt runners.
Move right and climb up to gain a small
precarious rock ledge and the only possible
rest position on the pitch. Pull straight up the
wall and climb a feint groove until moves right
lead to the final hanging groove (the most
noticeable feature observed from the ground).
Move up the groove, in an incredible position,
until it is possible to pull out right at its top.
Belay here or continue up easier rock to a
large ledge and nut belays.

Fear and Fascination—Description

Dove Crag is one of the most powerful crags
in the Lakes. Steep and high its overhanging
and unbroken nature offers a number of high
calibre routes that typify all that is fiercest
about the extreme grade. The centre of the
crag, the highest point, is recessed into a
corner groove and gives the line of Don
Whillans's Extol (E2). To the left is a formidable rock wall sweeping around a corner to
give first Hireath (E2) and then Dovedale
Groove (E1). To the right the wall bulges
steeply and is breached by Problem Child

**Looking to Dove Crag at the head of
Dovedale.**

82

Luke Steer makes an abseil retreat, the position of the vertical rope shows the incredibly overhanging nature of the crag on Fear and Fascination.

(E4) before the rock disintegrates into a great natural chimney fault. Immediately right of this is the traditional line of the crag, a remarkable first ascent for 1939, Jim Haggas's Hangover (HVS). Right of this the rock becomes much cleaner and more compact, the best and most solid on Dove, and begins to overhang dramatically. Here the top of the cliff impends over the base by some 30ft (9m). This is the North Buttress and is breached by the line of Fear and Fascination.

'Superb and unrelenting climbing—a really magnificent climb, probably the best modern line in the Lakes since Central Buttress' was the rather emotional comment I wrote in my diary after Rick Graham and I made the first ascent. It felt significantly easier than Broken Arrow (a route going leftwards from the same

start which we had climbed a month earlier), despite the latter's unfortunate two points of aid, and we graded it E4 with Rick arguing for a long time that it was only technically 5c—ah well, we were younger then.

It seemed for a couple of climbing years that Rick and I only ever went to one crag—Dove. This wasn't the case of course (Rick was very active in the Alps and I had begun to savour the best of sun rock in southern France—additionally we both climbed prolifically throughout Britain) but it was just that Dove is so dominating that everything else seemed to be subconsciously dismissed. It began with my passion to climb the North Buttress, then only breached by the aided route of the same name. After trying to interest various other climbers in sharing the challenge, with no success, I introduced Rick to it. There was an immediate and unanimous commitment to climb it. The bond forged in the iron towns of the north-east during earlier student days was re-established.

Firstly we took a ramp line leading magnificently leftwards through the most overhanging part of the crag. But the ramp was somewhat of an illusion. It simply took us to a barrier that forced two points of aid. Despite the fact that we both thought the climbing to be the best and hardest we had ever done, and the line a very natural one, the solution (using two points of aid) was not a totally satisfactory one.

It was Rick, in his analytically methodical way, who reasoned that a line to the right, although apparently blank and impossible, was the way to go. It was blank, yes, but it was not so steep or overhanging as the line of Broken Arrow and the nature of the rock meant there must be holds. Now Rick is always full of theories and because, like me, he is an engineer by profession, he inevitably puts them into practice. So it was here and we were soon back to attempt the overhanging wall yet again.

After various alternations of the lead I found myself on the traverse and mentally worked out a series of technical moves which I knew would unlock the solution, taking me across and onto slightly easier ground. Despite Rick's enthusiasm for me to do so it was not to be; on this occasion I could not summon the necessary complex practical requirements to motivate both mind and body sufficiently. On the ground I repeated the theory, hand change by hand change, finger flake hold for finger flake hold—we both believed it would work.

Rick successfully applied it and unlocked the psychological and physical barrier to what can be accurately described as a stupendous piece of rock climbing. It was in every way his pitch. Every move is a climbing move and the serious and hard moves above the precarious resting ledge require total commitment of both physical and mental effort.

When he reached the ledge on the first ascent, I urged him to take a belay, and so let me have a share of the action. Despite his reasoning, absolutely correctly, that this was totally illogical, he traversed left to take a rubbish belay over on the North Buttress route. The ropes hung miles out and the belay was dangerously inadequate. As he took in the rope I realised my folly and gave him the go-ahead to continue, which he did to great effect.

Pulling up from the ledge, with indifferent runners here and above, requires the rational approach—controlled explosive power that must last you from here to the top. It's no good shooting up regardless; there are no rests to be had. The technical difficulty hardly relents and the runner placements must be very carefully deciphered from a maze of complexities. Climbing up the final groove is like having all your birthdays and Christmases at once. Was there ever another position quite like this? You bridge in space, above a magnificent sea of overhanging difficulty and a myriad of technical exactness, where the precision of each move is imperative—a solid wall of unrelenting mental and physical effort. The route is aptly named Fear and Fascination.

There is something compelling about this overhanging rock and the line of Fear and Fascination, with the clean-cut final groove easily picked out from below, is probably the most attractive of the options. The best technique to reach the final groove is by no means certain but the grey-brown rock will be found to offer a surprisingly generous mixture of holds, both big and small.

Rick went back so I could photograph the route and Luke Steer proceeded to almost gain the final groove before succumbing to the unfavourably cold conditions. Al Phizacklea, patiently belaying their efforts (after which he went off to solo two new routes on the shoulder crags below—but that's another tale), described the route as 'visionary'. Weighing the evidence, all these years later, I think the comment is accurate. The climb will always remain a challenge but, most importantly, it is one which offers a spectrum of adventure and experience on Lakeland rock.

Luke Steer makes a big effort to reach the final groove on Fear and Fascination.

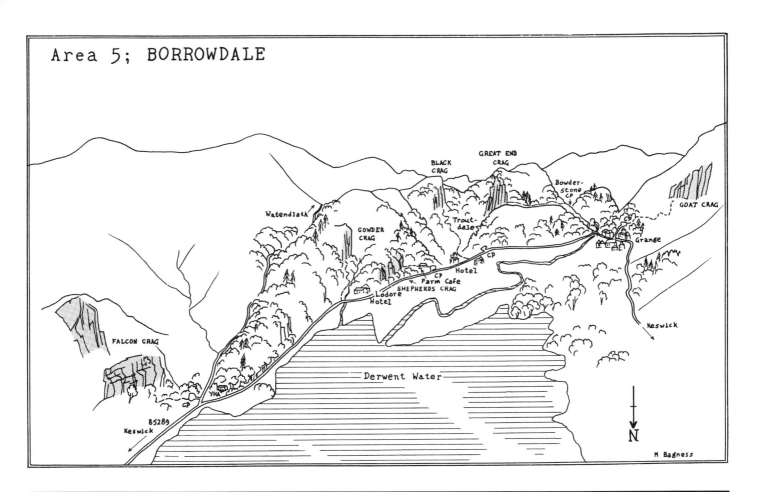

On the illustration: GREAT END CRAG, BLACK CRAG, Bowder-stone CP, GOAT CRAG, Watendlath, GOWDER CRAG, Trout-dale, Grange, CP, Hotel, Keswick, CP, Farm Cafe, SHEPHERDS CRAG, Lodore Hotel, FALCON CRAG, Derwent Water, YHA, CP, B5289 Keswick, N, M Bagness

BORROWDALE—LOWER FALCON CRAG

LOWER FALCON CRAG: Illusion, The Niche, Hedera Grooves.

Map Ref: NY 271205.

Guidebooks: *Rock Climbing in the Lake District* by Birkett, Cram, Eilbeck and Roper. *Borrowdale* (FRCC Guide) by D. Armstrong & R. Kenyon.

Attitude: Faces west.

Altitude: 500ft (150m).

Rock: Borrowdale Volcanic, tends to be rather slaty and there are some loose flakes.

Access: Falcon crags, upper and lower, stand above the road some two miles out from Keswick. Whilst it is possible to pull in below the crags and approach them directly from here it is better if one continues a hundred yards or so to fork left up the Watendlath road. After a few yards a cattle grid is crossed and immediately after this there is a sizeable car park on the left. A path leads up to the right end of Lower Falcon (10 minutes).

Descent: Walk across to the left end of the crag and follow down an easy scree gully.

Observations: Quick to get to and quick to dry this crag, once rather loose in places, offers a variety of steep and interesting routes.

LOWER FALCON CRAG: Illusion, The Niche and Hedera Grooves

ILLUSION: 145ft (44m), Hard Very Severe (5a).
First Ascent: P. Lockey, P. Ross (alt), 10 June 1956.
THE NICHE: 175ft (53m), E2 (5c).
First Ascent: A. Liddell, R. McHaffie, 20 August 1962.
HEDERA GROOVES: 135ft (41m), Mild Very Severe (4b).
First Ascent: P. Lockey. P. Ross (alt), 10 August 1956.
Location: Lower Falcon Crag, Borrowdale.

Illusion—Summary

Because it is usual to arrive at the right end of the crag the climbs will be described from right to left. Illusion starts nearly at the right end of the crag beneath a large overhang situated at the top. Start by the large tree.

1. 25ft (8m), (4b). Climb straight up to gain a stance and belays.

2. 100ft (30m), (5a). Climb a steep groove above, aiming up for the overhang until a large flake on the right can be gained. Make a slightly ascending traverse rightwards, crossing several grooves until a corner is reached beneath the right-hand end of the overhang. Swing around onto the wall and climb steeply to gain a ledge in a few feet.

3. 20ft (6m). Up the wall through the trees to reach the top.

The Niche—Summary

Roughly in the centre of the crag, about 35 yards left of Illusion there is a cavelike niche in the midst of the overhangs. Start beneath this.

1. 65ft (20m), (5c). There is a flake belay and the climb pulls through the overhanging rock just to its left. Continue up the wall to transfer onto the rib on the left. At its top there is a peg runner to the left and the object now is to traverse into the Niche which is 10ft (3m) to the right (crux).

Looking from below Falcon Crags across Derwentwater to Cat Bells and Causey Pike.

ILLUSION

THE NICHE

HEDERA
GROOVES

belay point

2. 40ft (12m), (5b). Move up the back of the Niche then traverse right across the rib and on to gain the obvious break through the overhangs. Up this to move right to a rock ledge and belay.

3. 70ft (21m), (4b). Step left, follow a gangway, then pull over a bulge, rightwards, to continue up the slabby wall to the top.

Hedera Grooves—Summary

Over to the left some way there is a great curtain of ivy. Start in a small bay just left of the ivy mass.

1. 80ft (24m), (4a). Up first to a grass ledge and then on to a bush. Traverse right to a groove and climb this to step left to gain the holly tree belay.

2. 55ft (17m), (4b). Climb the groove above the holly until the ramp can be followed, up leftwards, to the the top of the crag.

Illusion, The Niche and Hedera Grooves—Description

Paul Ross who extensively developed Borrow-

dale in the late 1950s and early 1960s, was under the impression that this crag would never capture the climbing public's imagination. He considered that the routes were generally too hard, too loose and too short! Fortunately he still persisted in instigating the development and succeeded in producing routes that are now recognised as modern classics. Today the crag is a good deal cleaner. Much of the loose rock has come away, occasionally with a climber still attached, and there is a mixture of climbs offering a variety of difficulty. Add to this the attractions of the short walk and the afternoon sunshine and it is now easy to understand why it has become one of the most popular of all the Lakeland crags.

Beneath the large overhangs, at the right end of the crag and hidden behind a large tree for some of the way, there lies a route of surprising interest and exposure. Illusion is one of those satisfying routes that only reveal their true virtue when climbed. The main pitch will suit the technically minded as it

Lower Falcon Crag showing Illusion, The Niche and Hedera Grooves.

weaves its way across bottomless grooves to assume a bold poition beneath the right end of the overhangs. There is an old peg here, and indifferent nuts can be found, but these and any other protection placed must be suitably extended, with proper care taken to clip the ropes correctly to prevent rope drag and the pulling of runners. Moves out from here are bold but the difficulties are short and holds you won't forget take you quickly to a belay.

Illusion tends to stay dry when most other routes in Borrowdale are out of the question. The overhangs above protect you from the rain and it is one of those routes that can generally be climbed all year round. Another consideration is that all the holds are extremely positive and on the only section that is usually wet, the wall where you emerge from the protective cover of the overhang, they are mostly incut. If you are one of those masochistic types prepared to brave cold fingers, this could be the route for an alternative Christmas Day.

A route of some controversy, because a disputed amount of aid was used when it was first put up, the Niche along with the Bludgeon on Shepherd's Crag, became one of the early test-pieces of Borrowdale climbing. Today, free of all the aid, it remains nothing less than a suberb climb—one of the best of its grade. Typically Ray McHaffie, one of the real characters of Borrowdale climbing, had just made an ascent of the route on the 25th anniversary of its first ascent, a few days before I photographed it for this book.

The challenge of the Niche does not require much scrutiny to pick it out. The recess glares tantalisingly down at you amidst a sea of overhangs. To force it in the early 1960s was a notable pioneering effort and in a number of ways the route generates a feeling of respect in much the same way as Vector does at Tremadog (Joe Brown's classic Welsh roadside route). Surprisingly Ado Liddell, now a top guide at Glenmore Lodge in the Cairngorms, did not go on to make many more new climbs whilst the other member of the team, Mac, probably holds the record for the actual number of first ascents in the valley.

Despite the presence of many more, harder climbs, the Niche will always be the best way up this section of rock—the undisputed line of the crag. It starts in much the same way as it continues, ascending overhanging rock. This however soon eases to vertical, and a rib to the left of the hanging niche leads to a position level with its base though some 10ft (3m)

horizontally away from it. This is the tricky bit and over the years it has repulsed many. A number of approaches can be taken but whichever you choose it is no place for the faint-hearted. Enough said, you must work out your own salvation!

The final pull leads to belays in the Niche itself and it's rather a curious position—a stance not large enough to be called a ledge, but a definite place of respite, yet offering only cold comfort from the overhangs above and below. From the top of this a traverse right, with nothing underneath and bulging rock above is a land of total steepness. The overhangs push you off whilst offering little in the way of obvious holds. But they are there and, despite the strenuousness, you must search them out. The feet, although essential to maintain you in the status quo, do their minimum to hold you in place.

This is an absorbing piece of climbing which does repay the considered approach. Arm strength and good footwork are both required—a demanding combination. As on the traverse of the first pitch there are a number of variations possible to accomplish it successfully. However it is not very far to reach the break, gain the groove above, and to seek those illusive jugs. Once reached, the rock ledge marks what for many is a not unwelcome change in the nature of the climbing and the wall above leads now comparatively easily to a flat top and distant belay.

The final route, Hedera Grooves, is a very pleasant climb and a lot easier than the others hereabouts. Even if you intend to move onto something much harder it's a good one to warm up on perhaps at the start of a season or as a prelude to something a bit more meaty— Spinup for example. It gives a worthwhile introduction to the nature of the climbing on Lower Falcon.

Above the tree belay, at the top of the first pitch, things start to liven up. A deep crack offers excellent protection before some awkward moves up the steep groove. However, beware; it's a real nut gobbler. A step left and a real gem of a sloping gangway leads leftwards and upwards. A steep bit up a little wall in a fine position leads to easy ground and the end of a rather nice route. But why make excuses, Ivy Grooves (Hedera is Latin for Ivy), positioned amicably between steep rock and luxuriant greenery, is a good enough climb even if you don't fancy anything else on Ross and Lockey's la'al Borrowdale crag.

Luke Steer on the edge of Hedera Grooves nearing the top of the 1st pitch with Keswick below.

BORROWDALE—SHEPHERD'S CRAG

Shepherd's Crag showing Little Chamonix and Ardus.

SHEPHERD'S CRAG: Little Chamonix, Ardus.
Map Ref: NY 264185.
Guidebooks: *Rock Climbing in the Lake District* by Birkett, Cramm, Eilbeck and Roper. *Borrowdale* (FRCC Guide) by D. Armstrong & R. Kenyon.
Attitude: Faces west.
Altitude: 300ft (90m).
Rock: Borrowdale volcanic, sound but rather polished.
Access: The crags lie immediately above the road some 3 miles (4km) from Keswick, sited on the left between the Lodore and Borrowdale Hotels. Parking is either in a small space (often blocked) directly below or by the track in the farmyard which is situated on the left just above the Borrowdale Hotel (generally enough room) where excellent value teas are served. The crag itself spreads across the hillside and consists of three main buttresses separated by scree; Little Chamonix Buttress on the right, Ardus Buttress approximately centre and Brown Slabs over to the left. If the approach from behind the farm is taken this leads to a stone wall below the first bit of crag. The Chamonix Buttress lies across the scree over to the left and Ardus across further scree (5 minutes from the farm).

Descent: For Little Chamonix go over to the right and either, find a gully leading down from where a left scramble leads below a wall of rock (Monolith Crack area), or continue traversing until the open fellside is reached. Descend this to reach a path which takes you back to the foot of the crag. For Ardus again go right to scramble down a gully to the scree break.

Observations: The quick-drying and easily accessible rocks that make up the various areas of Shepherd's Crag (Brown Slabs to the left, Ardus Buttress centre, Little Chamonix Buttress right with a smaller crag right again just above the stone wall) are hugely popular. To enjoy a modicum of peace and quiet it is therefore necessary to carefully select a sensible, off peak time to climb here. However, a little thought will be repaid for the setting and the climbing are both very fine.

LITTLE CHAMONIX: 220ft (67m), Very Difficult.
First Ascent: B. Beetham, 26 May 1946.
ARDUS: 130ft (40m), Hard Severe.
First Ascent: V. Veevers, H. Westmorland, P. Holt, 8 May 1948.
Location: Shepherd's Crag, Borrowdale.

Little Chamonix—Summary

Starts roughly in the centre of Chamonix Buttress about 40ft (12m) above and to the right of the lowest point of the crag. Over to the left there is a chimney groove with a tree in it and immediately to the right a large block with a dead tree growing out of it.

1. 100ft (30m). Climb the short crack to a ledge and then take a shallow scoop in the wall to gain the obvious groove above and slightly to the right. Climb this to near its top then step left and stand on the tip of a pinnacle to gain better holds on the ledge above. Move up to the tree belay.

2. 40ft (12m). Scramble up through the trees to a corner on the right. Above there are two distinct right-angled corner grooves.

3. 40ft (12m). Up the left hand groove and climb onto the table block at its top. From the table top, usually from a sitting position, step down rightwards onto the smooth slab (of the second groove) and traverse across to the right rib. Up this a few feet to the saddle belay. Nut belays above, small tree down to the right.

4. 40ft (12m). The steep wall above reaches the base of an impending wall (actually a pinnacle) and exposed moves lead across rightwards to a chimney. Up this and the short wall to the top. Take the tree belays well back, but extend them until you can see over the edge.

Ardus—Summary

The next buttress over the scree to the left of Little Chamonix has a distinct, unmistakably large corner up its centre. Start beneath some rightward-trending slabs about 40ft (12m) to the left of the lowest point of the buttress.

1. 130ft (40m) Move up rightwards to gain entry to the large corner. Climb this, steeply, using first the left wall and then the right—as the difficulties dictate. A ledge and block belay is reached some 25ft (8m) below the top.

2. 35ft (11m). Ascend left across the slab using the flake crack to reach the first vertical crack. Use this to gain the top.

Little Chamonix and Ardus— Description

Despite the fact that Shepherd's is frighteningly popular it does retain its own characteristic charm. The popularity is easy to understand; it's the most accessible of all crags, it dries quickly and there is interest for both rock athlete and novice. Its other qual-

Jon Rigby on the superbly steep last pitch of Little Chamonix with Derwentwater beyond.

Dave Belgrove on the left wall of the corner of Ardus.

ing hills. On days such as these you will discover good evidence supporting the argument that Borrowdale is the most beautiful of all Lakeland valleys.

If one single pioneer could be identified as doing the most to popularise the Borrowdale valley then the indefatigable Bentley Beetham would be high on the list. He first discovered Shepherd's Crag, along with C. D. Frankland, when he climbed Brown Slabs Arete in 1922. Such was the slow pace of development that it was he who returned some *twenty-four years* later, in 1946, to put up the next climb and resume exploration of the crag. This time, however, the word got out and the routes began to fall thick and fast.

It was on a May day during that summer of rediscovery in 1946 that Bentley put up, solo, what I consider to be his best ever route. Like only the greatest works of art, Little Chamonix is something that you can experience time and again without ever growing tired of it. From the road below, above the Borrowdale Hotel, the top pitch is easily the most eye-catching line on Shepherd's. Of course there are times when the route is bound to be festooned with other parties but with common sense and prudence it is still possible to climb alone. However at the peak periods, particularly during a public holiday, you could be excused for thinking that a head-torch would be necessary to find solitude.

Despite the small scale of the crag the route runs to some 220ft (67m) and gives three interesting pitches (plus one of scrambling) of some variety. There is exposure to be found and some of the positions obtained are unique! The first pitch, although generally straightforward, does not lack interest and standing on the razor-edged pinnacle to reach the belay ledge will test the beginner's qualities of balance.

Above the tree ledge the route follows the left-hand, right-angled groove capped by the table block. Crossing the table top and transferring into the the smooth groove on the right is a problem that baffles many. Probably the best technique is to sit down and shuffle across until the feet can friction the steep wall of the groove on the right. A good runner can be placed at the back of the table top. Making progress up the groove and over to the rib is yet another story!

At the end of this section, in keeping with the spirit of the route, it is usual to take a saddle belay astride the rib. A ledge and small tree down to the right offer a non-sporting alternative! Remarkably impending for the

ities are probably best enjoyed on the rare quiet days—if you are lucky enough to find one.

The rock, although short, is always entertaining. Sometimes it is rough and pocketed, sometimes smooth, flaky and brittle. In summer the setting is most exquisite. You climb from a cool green canopy of leaves to view the clear sky and nearby Derwentwater, a tranquil sapphire nestling beneath the surround-

grade the last pitch sets the seal on a deservably popular route. Photographed from the flat terrace above, cantilevered so that you can sit with legs dangling in space and nothing at all in front to impair the shot, the picture is dramatic. For from here you can't see the munificent nature of the handholds.

Ardus, or more correctly Audus, is an exciting and solid route first taking the sweeping corner crack and then moving boldly and delicately across a steep and exposed wall. I recently met up with Vince Veevers, who led the first ascent, and he filled me in on some interesting facts. Firstly that the name Ardus currently used in the guidebook (mine included) is in fact a spelling mistake and that the original name given was Audus—his wife-to-be's maiden name. Well at this stage the name Ardus is so familiar and committed to the climbing vocabulary that I think it must stick even if it is by default. Whatever the name the climb is a fine one and that is the most important consideration.

The long first pitch is quite involved and it is quite easy to make it more difficult than is necessary. Whilst the runners are good if the crack is taken absolutely unswervingly, over the block and straight up, it will prove both strenuous and precarious in places. Better to utilise the walls on either side; sometimes the left, sometimes the right and sometimes bridging—but you must discover the best way for yourself.

Crossing the exposed wall with no protection from the security and confines of the ledge in the corner can be a heart-thumping business; technical too. The question is do you go high and use the footholds in the vague flake crack? If you do you will find a distinct lack of handholds to move left with when the flake crack dries. Or do you go low and friction with the feet? The traverse finishes when a thin crack is reached which is then climbed, not without some excitement, to the security of the belay ledge. The crack is steep, if short, and even these final few moves place the climb strongly in the Hard Severe category.

Vic showed me some photographs taken by the third man on the rope, P. Holt. There was a massive tree with great gangling naked roots, fastened into what must now be the belay ledge in the corner. Nonchalantly standing in the roots belaying as Vic leads for the first time across the flake crack, is Colonel H. Westmorland. Their rope is hemp and the belay taken by running it over the shoulder. It was in fact the Colonel (Rusty) who disco-

vered the line and pointed Vic up it. Asking Vic how he found the climbing on the day, I wasn't altogether surprised, judging by his record elsewhere, when he said: 'To tell you the truth I was disappointed, I felt a little let down because the flake crack was a lot easier than I thought it was going to be. I was keyed up for a very hard problem and it went too easily!'

You won't feel let down I can assure you for the now treeless Audus is a real belter.

Dave Belgrove climbing the corner of the 1st pitch of Ardus.

BORROWDALE—BLACK CRAG

BLACK CRAG: The Mortician, Prana.
Map Ref: NY 263174.
Guidebooks: *Rock Climbing in the Lake District* by Birkett, Cram, Eilbeck and Roper. *Borrowdale* (FRCC Guide) by D. Armstong and R. Kenyon.
Attitude: Faces north-west.
Altitude: 800ft (244m).
Rock: Borrowdale Volcanic.
Access: Up the Borrowdale road from Keswick (3.5 miles, 6km) past the Borrowdale Hotel (on left) a right-angled bend has Derwent View House on the right and the track leading to Black Crag on the left. Just past the bend, on the left, there is a purpose-made car park. Follow the track to a gate and on through the field of Troutdale (old trout ponds over on the left) until one can break left over the stream and climb directly through the woods to the bottom of the crag (20 minutes).

Descent: A path leads up and rightwards across the hill to contour above the right wing of the crag until a worn rock slab drops to a stone wall and footpath which traverses down beneath the crag.

Observations: Left of the highest and central most part of the crag is a steep wall with its base submerged in a sea of trees. The two climbs described here are situated in this area.

Labels on image: Crux, PRANA, (Base obscured by trees), THE MORTICIAN, belay point

BLACK CRAG: The Mortician and Prana

THE MORTICIAN: 320ft (98m), Hard Very Severe (5a).
First Ascent: B. Thompson, W. A. Barnes (alt), 7 August 1969.
PRANA: 140ft (43m), E3 (5c).
First Ascent: P. Gommersal, 4 September 1977.
Location: Black Crag, Borrowdale.

The Mortician—Summary

One arrives at the lowest point of the crag and the start of this route lies up a slab just a few feet left of this.

1. 100ft (30m), (4b). Climb directly up the slab to a ledge (there is a flake crack to the right—Troutdale Pinnacle Direct). Step left and ascend a dirty corner to a ledge and birch tree belays.

2. 140ft (43m), (5a). From the right climb the clean wall of the rectangular groove (overlap above) moving up leftwards to enter the larger groove above. Up this until awkward moves out right enable the straight crack to be gained. Climb this and then over easier broken ground to a stance where the wall again steepens.

3. 75ft (23m), (4c). Enter the shallow groove on the left (a finger traverse leads rightwards but this is the line of the Superdirect) up this, over a bulge, and up the easier-angled continuation above until a bold looking traverse leads back right, across the wall, onto the edge. Follow the arete to the top (final pitch of Troutdale Pinnacle).

Prana—Summary

To the left again a wide dirty gully runs up through the crag. Start left of the tree-filled gully below a slab. Climb easily up the slab (invariably wet) to a ledge and tree belay.

1. 140ft (43m), (5c). Climb the wall taking a dark streak right of the tree belay to gain the halfway roof. Traverse right a few feet and pull over the roof, on small holds, through the little break (the gully is about 10ft (3m) to the right). Take the wall fairly directly until a step

Black Crag showing The Mortician and Prana.

left can be made onto a rock ledge. Good runners (approximately Rock 3 size) in a diagonal crack up to the left. Step right and up the bulging wall. The crux is a long reach to better handholds from a thin break. Where the angle relents somewhat step left, then up to an easy slab and tree belay. It is usual to abseil from this although easy, mossy, climbing leads left from here and up to the top in about another 50ft (15m).

The Mortician and Prana—Description

The left-hand side of Black Crag is a good place to climb in the late afternoon or evening, when it begins to catch the sun. The best place to stop and view the crag is from the meadows of Troutdale, as on arrival at its foot the overhanging nature and proliferation of trees make it impossible to see much crag detail.

The Mortician, although it was not climbed until 1969, is one of the most logical and direct routes on this stretch of rock. Perhaps it needed some gardening which initially deterred would-be ascensionists for today the long second pitch is a glaringly obvious line. A wide groove leads directly to a proud-looking vertical handjam crack.

Luckily the first pitch is better than it looks. Just as well! It is the second pitch that takes on immediate interest. Firstly it moves up a steep barrier wall to gain the groove proper. This is followed until at about half height an inconsequential-looking move rightwards to exit the groove proves to be the crux. Just above this, the handjam crack is actually a bit of a cheat—much to the relief of Mark Greenbank, soloing the route for my cameras, who being a Lakes climber doesn't handjam. It's full of hidden holds and it's quite possible to get away without using a single jam.

This second pitch, although quite long, giving solid climbing, does have plenty of places to rest and stand in balance. Additionally the protection is frequent and of suitable quality. Moves over easier ground lead to a last pitch which is reasonably absorbing and magnificently exposed.

From below Prana always looks ghastly. Black-stained slabs and the similarly stained wall above give the appearance that they are constantly oozing water. Fortunately this is usually a deception and the wall above the first little tree ledge will be found to be snuff dry.

Once launched onto the wall the climb immediately becomes absorbing and remains so until the belay tree is reached some 140ft (43m) above. Small wires can be placed at intervals and some good runners wangled in on first arrival at the break. The pull through the roof on very small handholds gives a taste of what is to come. Above, the the first objective is a rock ledge some way up to the left. This ledge is shared by Grand Alliance (an equally fine route) and it is wise to place the bomb-proof wire runners that can be found in a diagonal crack a few feet up to the left (approximately Rock 3 size). Stepping right to continue up the wall brings the distinct crux quickly to hand. It pays dividends to sort out the footwork here using the small edges to

Mark Greenbank on The Mortician moving right from the first groove on the 2nd pitch.

Mark Greenbank reaches the overhangs of Prana.

get the feet as high as possible. From two small crimping handholds it is necessary to reach a long way for a better handhold and once reached, a few upward moves bring some welcome respite.

This is a very pleasant wall climb in the modern idiom, reasonably sustained and with a distinct crux. It is technically demanding without being desperate and all the better because of it.

I first climbed Prana with Ken Forsythe, the day after I put up a route called Fall Out on Esk Buttress. In my diary I note that I recorded Prana to be 'E2 and straightfor-

ward'. At that time, Prana felt a full technical two grades easier. Recently, watching Mark Greenbank and Luke Steer at close quarters, I felt equally positive that it must warrant E3.

The point is that whilst grades may be fickle and the apparent difficulty can vary with a number of factors, it is the amount of enjoyment and personal satisfaction you derive from climbing a route that is the lasting factor. The intrinsic quality of the fingertip wall climbing on Prana cannot seriously be disputed—let that be your criterion for selection. Have a good climb.

BORROWDALE—GREATEND CRAG

Great End with Nagasaki Grooves.

GREATEND CRAG: Nagasaki Grooves.
Map Ref: NY 260170.
Guidebooks: *Rock Climbing in the Lake District* by Birkett, Cram, Eilbeck and Roper. *Borrowdale* (FRCC Guide) by D. Armstrong and R. Kenyon.
Attitude: Faces north-west.
Altitude: 750ft (230m).
Rock: Borrowdale Volcanic.
Access: On the main road some way past Grange there is the Bowderstone Quarry car park on the left. Follow the path out left from the car park to gain a shoulder below the crag.

When the crag becomes visible take a line directly towards it (20 minutes).
Descent: This is best taken to the right of the crag.
Observations: Once hidden beneath a cloak of lichen and vegetation this large crag has been subject to intense gardening activity. A number of good routes emerged from beneath the greenery but none finer than the route, which actually pre-dated most of the heavy gardening exploits, described here.

GREATEND CRAG: Nagasaki Grooves

NAGASAKI GROOVES: 300ft (91m), E4 (6b).
First Ascent: C. Read, J. Adams (some aid), 24 July 1972. P. Livesey (free solo) 22 June 1974.
Location: Greatend Crag, Borrowdale.

Nagasaki Grooves—Summary

Roughly in the centre of the crag is a long continuous corner (Greatend Corner HVS) and to the left of this there is a pinnacle at the base of a crag. This is the starting point.

1. 105ft (32m), (5b). Climb up the pinnacle to gain the white corner. Continue to move left over an overlap to gain a more distinct corner. Climb this to step left into the next corner. Proceed up this over a bulge until it eases. Take a belay below the crack.

2. 150ft (46m), (6b). Take the slab on the left until it becomes a wall. Step slightly left, then right, and climb the wall and grooves until the smooth groove above can be reached. Up this with a high step (crux) on the right wall until it is possible to make a short traverse left. Climb over the bulge to another overlap. Continue directly up the groove to a small ledge and belay.

3. 45ft (14m), (4b). Continue up the recess, vague crack, to the finishing ledges and tree belays.

Nagasaki Grooves—Description

'Probably the best pitch in Borrowdale, youth,' concluded Colin Downer coiling the ropes at the bottom. Long, technical, steep, unrelenting were just a few of the applicable adjectives that sprang to mind as I assessed his spontaneity. 'It's tremendous climbing,' I concurred weighing the evidence. 'Maybe it is.'

There is a large boulder on the heavily brackened shoulder beneath the cliff, by the side of the tourist path. Viewed from here in the afternoon sun, when the shadowed grooves are thrown into sharp relief against the mass of the crag, it is the line of Nagasaki that becomes the most inspirational. From elsewhere, and at other times of the day, it is difficult to appreciate the quality of bumbly Bentley Beetham's Greatend Crag.

It was left to someone of inquisitive pioneering instinct to investigate and realise the modern potential of this large, steep piece of Borrowdale rock. Colin Read and John Adams were the team. At that time there were few who had both the in-depth knowledge of the many extreme possibilities com-

bined with the ability and confidence to climb them. These two important Lakeland pioneers did. In many ways it was this climbing partnership that pointed the way for the great free climbing boom that hit the Lake District in the 1970s.

Because Read was called to Japan (hence

Colin Downer above the first crux groove of Nagasaki Grooves.

Colin Downer completing the crux sequence of moves and utilising positive holds that lead to the final difficult groove on Nagasaki.

the name) the route was ascended from bottom to top in rather a rush. Scrupulously honest about their activities, they recorded five pegs for aid. Soon after that, the book of rules changed very fast, with Pete Livesey doing much to rewrite it. Whilst abseil cleaning (hammering off loose rock and wire brushing to remove the moss lichen and other sundry vegetation), and even practising the route from an abseil rope whilst noting the best nut placements, became the approved practice the final ascent had to be done all 'free' to obtain the accolade of both the climbing public and the press. The means to the end was no longer subject to question, so long as the end product was a free ascent.

Examining many of Pete Livesey's first ascents it is obvious that any recorded climb employing aid became a target for his free climbing ambition. He wasn't so much finding new rock, or new climbs, as applying his new free climbing rules to existing climbs. The end result was a series of beautiful modern free routes typified by the free ascent of Nagasaki Grooves.

The history books[1] will record that Pete made the first free ascents of both Nagasaki Grooves and Dry Gasp (E3, 6a—on Upper Falcon Crag) solo (though with a back-rope) on 22nd June 1984. An impressive statistic even compared with his other achievements of this, his most dynamic year of free climbing activity. However, they will relate little of the excellent quality of climbing to be experienced on Nagasaki Grooves, hence I can justifiably divulge some of this detail.

The first pitch, common with Banzai Pipeline, is well worth climbing, with the added bonus that if you don't fancy launching off on the big pitch, you can continue up its corner cracks and still have the satisfaction and enjoyment of climbing a three-star HVS. The main pitch of Nagasaki Grooves is something else! Not particularly difficult by the extreme standards of today it gives rewarding climbing that does not relent for one inch. Protection, generally small wire placements, is adequate without being generous.

The first bulging wall gives a few 6a moves to reach the groove proper. Making a high step on the left wall, where the smooth walls above overlap those below, constitutes the crux. A technical and precarious move, careful observation and use of the feet will pay dividends here. It is fortunately adequately protected. Many have been tempted to try elswhere, by tackling the rounded holdless arete to the right for example, but I don't yet know of any successful variations.

Moves left, possible rest, and then steeply up again lead to another square-cut vertical groove. The protection in the groove itself is poor, and trust must be put in the runners now well below the feet. Colin reckons this is the crux for him. A few interesting moves, a good deal of commitment, and a long reach lead to the end of the major difficulties. From here it is just a short hike to the top.

1. *Lakeland's Greatest Pioneers*, by Bill Birkett, Robert Hale 1980.

BORROWDALE—GOAT CRAG

GOAT CRAG: Praying Mantis, Bitter Oasis.
Map Ref: NY 265165.
Guidebooks: *Rock Climbing in the Lake District* by Birkett, Cram, Eilbeck and Roper. *Borrowdale* (FRCC Guide) by D. Armstrong, R. Kenyon.
Attitude: Faces north-east.
Altitude: 1000ft (300m).
Rock: Borrowdale Volcanic, mossy in places.
Access: Driving from Keswick turn right over the narrow bridge into the tiny hamlet of Grange. A narrow road (signposted unfit for cars) leads off to the left and terminates at a campsite. Before this is reached the track narrows, just after it forks. Take the left fork. It is best to park by the wall at this point. From the campsite meadow take the stile onto the fell path and follow this to where it crosses the stream. It is best to keep low and traverse across left following the track along the wall. This rises

to reach the left end of the crag, then a diagonal rake leads back up right. The climbs described are situated on the highest buttress on the far right, before the crag becomes completely bestrewn with trees (20 minutes).
Descent: Abseil from the central tree (silver birch) if no one is climbing below—50-m ropes *just reach*—or go further right, to abseil just right of Bitter Oasis. The latter is probably the best alternative and avoids problems with anyone climbing below.
Observations: The climbs chosen are situated on the Great Buttress of Goat Crag and it is only on close acquaintance that the true nature of the place can be appreciated. Ignore first impressions formed from a distance—there is much more rock, steep and of good quality, than is first apparent.

Looking to Goat Crag from the Bowderstone car park.

GOAT CRAG: Praying Mantis and Bitter Oasis

PRAYING MANTIS: 260ft (79m), E1 (5b).
First Ascent: L. Brown, J. S. Bradshaw, 30 May 1965.
Bitter Oasis: 170ft (52m), E3 (5c).
First Ascent: P. Livesey, J. Sheard, 12 May 1974.
Location: Great Buttress, Goat Crag, Borrowdale.

Goat Crag showing the routes of Praying Mantis and Bitter Oasis.

GOAT CRAG

The Bitter Oasis

BITTER OASIS

PRAYING MANTIS

belay point

Praying Mantis—Summary

This main buttress is known as the Great Buttress and the distinct corner crack bounding its left side is the distinctive line of the route.

1. 260ft (79m), (5b). Straight up the square-cut groove to stand on a large flake on its left side. Pull back into the crack and climb it to gain a niche at its top. The section gaining entry to the niche constitutes the crux. Move out left across the wall and step up right to gain the slab above. This leads to a tree belay.

2. 50ft (15m), (4c). The line leads up and across leftwards. Traverse the wall to a distinct groove. Up this for 15ft (5m) until a step right gives a stance below block overhangs.

3. 135ft (41m), (4c). Traverse delicately right to a small ledge (possible belay). Move up diagonally rightwards, then more directly to a break in the overlap. This leads to a shallow scoop directly taking the wall above. It is advisable to seek low runners because the wall is somewhat lacking in protection. Follow this until it is easier to step left following the slab to a dirty terrace and tree belays.

Bitter Oasis—Summary

To the right of the Great Buttress there is a tree ledge some 20ft (6m) up. Start from this ledge.

1. 90ft (27m), (5c). From the tree on the left-hand end of the ledge climb up leftwards until moves back right lead to the base of a distinct groove. Climb the groove, passing an old peg runner near the top, to pull through the bulges onto the slab above—the Bitter Oasis. Trend steeply rightwards and up to a ledge and nut belays. It is best to keep low on the belays ensuring the nuts are correctly loaded to keep them in place.

2. 80ft (24m), (5c). Step up and leftwards onto the wall. A peg used to protect the next section but it has now gone and the climbing is somewhat serious. Traverse leftwards, good tiny footholds low down, until a standing position can be gained below a downward-pointing spike on the edge. Small nut runners can be arranged here. Step left and climb the wall, there is an old bolt runner after a few feet. Above this, climb directly up the bulging wall with good inconspicuous finger-holds, until a ledge and respite is gained. Continue up more easily, leftwards, to the silver birch tree belays.

Praying Mantis and Bitter Oasis—Description

It was Les Brown, one of Lakeland's most remarkable pioneers, who opened up Goat Crag by literally digging Praying Mantis out of the hillside. It is hard to believe that this route was once swathed in grass and vegatation for it is now not only clean but polished. The climb distinctly bears the Brown hallmark of quality and is continually interesting despite the fact that the major difficulties occur in the first 50ft (15m).

The crux is more akin to a gritstone chimney or crack problem than the type of climbing one would usually associate with the Lake District. Today it is distinctly polished and sound technique is required to execute it efficiently. One must gain a precarious position before it is possible to reach into the crack to either place a runner (small friend) or begin to handjam. Good footwork also helps here and all in all it is a really absorbing piece of climbing.

I was engaged in cleaning my camera lens when Mark Greenbank launched into his first attack, straight into a layback up the edge. I couldn't believe that anyone would even attempt to do this when the obvious technique is to jam in the back of the groove. I was so shocked that the camera lay dormant, most unprofessional. Sure enough within a few seconds of starting he was off, flying through the air to end dangling with his head a mere nothing from the big flake.

'Mark, you've got to learn to jam,' was the only comment I could mutter, heart pounding. Working on the theory that it's always worse to watch than to take a fall, I waited for a repeat of the action. Sure enough after a five-second rest the lad was starting again. This time he pretended to jam, lest I should remonstrate with him further and at least put his hands somewhere near the crack. However, I'm certain it was pure youthful exuberance that shot him up into the niche and nothing to do with his jamming technique.

Mark Greenbank launches off on the crux of Praying Mantis.

Martin Bagness traversing the wall rightwards on the 3rd pitch of Praying Mantis.

Although from below the space walk left and the hanging slab above look more difficult than the niche, they aren't. There is now nothing as technically difficult, but the climbing remains consistently absorbing as the size and position of the buttress begin to assert themselves. It is patently obvious that you are taking the easiest, inescapable, line up a very steep piece of rock.

A word of warning. The top pitch can be quite a long run out, without any protection, particularly if conditions are less than perfect. It is worth placing the good runners that can be readily found in the first 30ft (9m) of

Mark Greenbank finds that moves up from the edge on Bitter Oasis become increasingly strenuous.

vertical ascent. These lead to a little overlap (after the traverse horizontally right) and afterwards it is difficult to get anything worthwhile. Perhaps this is how it should be; it helps you appreciate the exposure a little more!

The start to Bitter Oasis gives a distinctly vegetated appearance but this, as on countless Borrowdale climbs, is an illusion. Immediately you launch off, the climbing is evenly sustained; technical wall climbing for move after move—pitch after pitch; quality climbing, something to get excited about.

It used to be that both pitches were pretty evenly balanced in difficulty, technically there is still little to choose between the two. But the protection peg has gone from the wall above the stance. In consequence the first 30ft (9m) or so of the second pitch are now extremely serious. It is important to make the belay a good one and accept the challenge. But this pushes the grade from comfortable mild E3 to hard E3.

From the tree ledge it may be difficult to assume the concentration necessary. The tree towering immediately behind belies the urgency of the situation. However the moves across and up to gain the distinct groove rapidly bring home the character of the climbing about to be experienced. Above the old peg the groove dies in a bulging wave of rock shielding entry onto what appears to be an easy-angled slab above. Steepening moves, always with adequate holds appearing just when you absolutely need them, lead to a pull through the bulges onto the expected easy slab and respite. Only it isn't a slab, and there isn't any respite. The apparent slab is found on arrival to be a continuingly technical wall, the expected rest only a fanciful illusion—your Bitter Oasis.

Further steep climbing bearing slightly rightwards leads to the stance proper. Out left there is a really big drop. Traverse across above it, on tiny holds and with no protection, until a standing position is reached right on the edge, below an overlap. The traverse is best achieved low and microscopic examination will reveal a thumb-size footswopping hold which makes the traverse comfortably less than desperate. Do arrange protection here for the old bolts you aim for and clip are not in pristine condition. Above, the wall leans out and bulges. If it wasn't for the fact that you are already standing in the middle of nothing, at the end of a tricky traverse, you could be excused for wanting out. But there isn't any out, only up. Relish it, it's really great climbing.

Mark Greenbank traverses out left across the wall from the top of the pod on Praying Mantis.

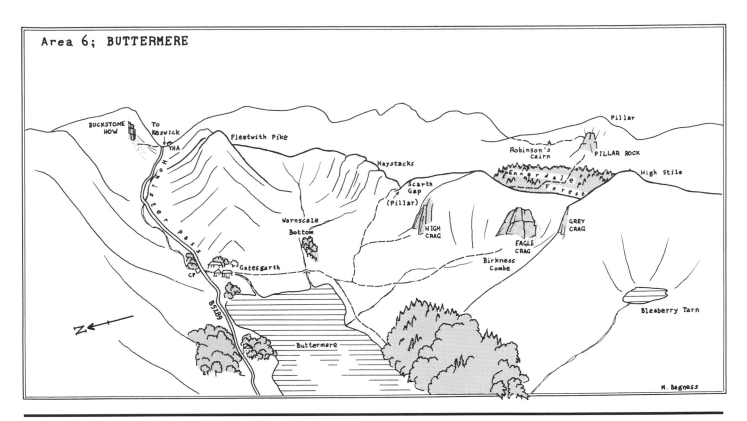

M. Bagness

BUTTERMERE—PILLAR ROCK

PILLAR ROCK: North-West Climb/Rib and Slab Climb (Combination), New West Climb.
Map Ref: NY 172123
Guidebooks: *Rock Climbing in the Lake District* by Birkett, Cram, Eilbeck and Roper. *Pillar Group* (FRCC Guide) by A. G. Cram.
Altitude: 2,000ft (610m).
Rock: Rhyolite—hard and rough, lichenous in places.
Access: There are three choices of approach: from Ennerdale (unless you are based on the west coast this is a long drive from anywhere and remains a long walk if the gate is locked); from Wasdale (the traditional approach and a good way to reach Pillar); from Buttermere (arguably the most enjoyable approach).
Ennerdale: Most useful to climbers based on the West Cumbria coast but since the Forestry Commision have begun locking the gates firstly under Bowness Knott just after the unmetalled road begins and further on by the hostel it is now a somewhat long approach (2 hours).
Wasdale: A good way to reach the rock taking the famous High Level Route to Robinson's Cairn. From the Wasdale Head take the track leading up Mosedale and then up onto the ridge via Black Sail Pass. Follow the ridge towards Pillar until it steepens, where there is a track (cairn) branching off to the right—this is the High Level Route leading to Robinson's Cairn and the view to Pillar Rock (2 hours).

Buttermere: This always seems the friendliest approach to Pillar despite the two ascents, one from Buttermere and then from Ennerdale. Start from Gatesgarth and proceed up to the top of Scarth Gap. Shortly after the summit there is an ill-defined path breaking off the main path to the right (don't miss this). It traverses down through the forest to a footbridge over the River Lisa. On the far side, above the bridge a signed path leads one up a forestry break to open ground. Traverse right to find the most well worn path leading directly to Pillar Rock. There is another break further to the right and this may be taken to find the main path directly above (2 hours).
Observations: Although I have included it in the Buttermere area, because this gives probably the most popular approach, Pillar Rock is situated above Ennerdale—between the Wasdale and Buttermere valleys. It is a traditional crag, one of the most striking in the Lake District, which because of its relative remoteness and impressive form still retains an air which commands reverance. Despite its rather dark aspect and often licheny rock it is a crag with a devoted following for whom there is simply no finer ground for climbing.

Careful note should be taken of the approaches and descents detailed for each climb. Pillar is a large mountain crag and its seriousness, particularly in poor weather, should not be underestimated. The best descent from the top of the rock is by abseil into the gap (Jordan Gap) between it and the buttress of Pisgah on the side of Pillar Mountain (but in any case scrambling of at least moderate difficulty is involved). If the steeper descent is taken down West Cove Gully (to the right of the rock) it must be realised that this leads into the vertical ground of West Waterfall which must be circumnavigated, as described below, to reach the Green Ledge Traverse—you cannot safely go straight down. Alternatively if the easier descent across the Shamrock Traverse is to be taken (this follows a line above the rocks to the left of the pillar) it is essential that one climbs up the hillside of Pillar Mountain above Pisgah buttress to find the well defined traverse. Do not descend the scree from either Jordan Gap or from behind Pisgah as this leads into the top of the vertical rift of Walker's Gully (so called because of the unfortunate who did just this and fell to his death). The sketch details the important points and this should be studied until the important topographical features are familiar.

Looking above the pines of Ennerdale to the Pillar Rock.

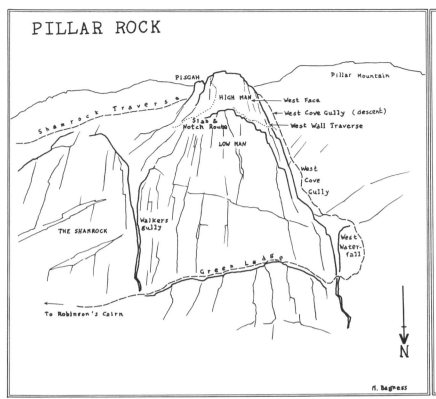

PILLAR ROCK

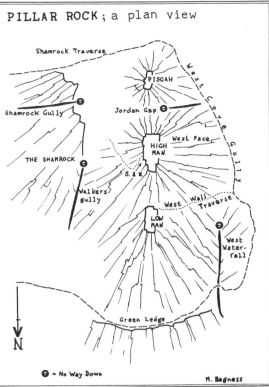

PILLAR ROCK; a plan view

⊖ = No Way Down

M. Bagness

PILLAR ROCK: North-West Climb/Rib and Slab Climb (Combination)

NORTH-WEST CLIMB: 445ft (136m), Mild Very Severe (4b).

First Ascent: F. W. Botterill, L. J. Oppenheimer, A. Botterill, J. H. Taylor, 8 June 1906.

Location: Initially taking the right side of the North Face of Low Man and then continuing to climb the West Face of Pillar Rock, Ennerdale.

Attitude: Initially faces north then west.

Access: If approached from below (from Buttermere or Ennerdale) the main buttress forms the towering pillar itself—this is known as Low Man. To the left a great chimney rift (Walker's Gully) splits Low Man off from the rocks to its left (the Shamrock) and from its foot a distinct ledge—Green Ledge—traverses across rightwards beneath Low Man. North-West Climb starts from the right-hand end of this ledge (above 300ft (90m) of more broken rocks below).

Descent and Access to the West Face:
Immediately above the top of the route a traverse line leads over to the right to make a descending undulating traverse across into the gully on the right. This is known as the West Wall Traverse (and is the bottom section of the Old West Route) and includes easy climbing, perhaps moderate in difficulty. This takes you

into a scree-filled gully below the magnificent west face and it is recommended that a further climb, in this case Rib and Slab Climb, is done to take you right to the very top of Pillar Rock. (This summit buttress is known as High Man.) Alternatively if you wish to descend to the foot of the North-West Climb directly then go down the gully keeping to the left side (looking out). As it steepens follow the well worn path taking the rocky rib to the left (looking out) of the gully. Again the rocks steepen and it is necessary now to traverse across (rightwards looking out) and down into the gully (vertical waterfall above and below) then climb immediately up out of it to gain a descending traverse to the end of the Green Ledge—the start of the climb. The path is well worn, if a little indistinct, but great care should be exercised not to descend down the gully from where it steepens because it then becomes a series of vertical waterfalls. There is no safe way down the gully below the Green Ledge. If in doubt it is wise to examine the descent before commencing the climb.

RIB AND SLAB CLIMB: 300ft (90m), Severe (4a!).

First Ascent: C. F. Holland, H. M. Kelly, C. G. Crawford, 29 July 1919.

Location: West Face of High Man, Pillar Rock.

Attitude: Faces west.

Access: If North-West Climb is done first then follow the above details. If it is intended to climb only on the West Face then one ascends up into West Cove Gully from the end of the Green Ledge reversing the descent details given above (see New West Climb for specific detail).

Descent: From the summit of Pillar Rock (High Man) the most straightforward descent is by abseiling into in the gap (Jordan Gap) just beyond the cairn. With a little examination a suitable, if small, polished boss will be discovered and the doubled ropes can easily be pulled from this. It is about 40ft (12m) to the bed of the gap. Once in the gap it is possible to climb out rightwards (looking at the far wall) then up to the top of Pisgah at about moderate in standard—but take care this is extremely slippery if wet. From here scramble down into the notch between Pisgah and Pillar Mountain. Either continue down rightwards into West Cove Gully and the foot of the west face then proceed down to Green Ledge and the foot of North-West Climb as described above or (an easier descent to be recommended if there is no requirement to retrieve the rucksack from beneath the west face) ascend up the hillside until a distinct track can be followed leading across leftwards (the Shamrock Traverse). This takes you easily across and down to the far left side of the Pillar complex and gives the easiest descent.

PILLAR ROCK — NORTH FACE LOW MAN

Le Coin

WEST COVE

WALKER'S GULLY

NORTH—WEST CLIMB

GREEN LEDGE

○ belay point

Pillar Rock showing the North-West Climb.

Exiting from the vertical wall above Le Coin on the 5th pitch on North-West Climb.

The balancey move up the nose of North-West Climb to gain the Perched Block on pitch 6.

North-West Climb—Summary

From the right end of Green Ledge a short ramp leading to a grassy ledge gives an inauspicious start to an excellent climb.

1. 70ft (21m), (3c). Take the ramp rightwards to the ledge. Go up the chimney above until an exposed traverse left across a delicate slab (Three-Step Traverse) leads to a ledge and belay below a step chimney crack.

2. 55ft (17m). Climb the corner chimney making full use of the wall behind. After it narrows to a crack skill in handjamming is a decided advantage. Follow it to corner and belay.

3. 50ft (15m), (3c). Climb the short rock wall to the left (the crest of a rib is now just to your left) then take a crack up the slab until scrambling leads to easier ground and a commodious ledge—belay beneath the next distinct wall of rock.

4. 30ft (9m), (3b). This bit detours around the steep hard short groove that leads directly on the buttress above by moving first right and then back left to just above the belay. If the runners are suitably placed and extended it can be combined with the pitch above. Move right into a corner and climb this until a few moves lead leftwards to a little ledge and sharp flake belay.

5. 60ft (18m), (4a). Move round the corner on the left then follow the steep shallow groove passing a bulge and two ledges to a recess (Le Coin). Move up the vertical wall on the right to reach a grass ledge. Go up and left to a ledge and belay.

6. 20ft (6m), (4a). Up the corner then step left to a very delicate nose of rock. Balance up this to gain a large perched block (take care) and stand on it to belay (Block Ledge).

7. 80ft (24m), (4a). Move left and climb over rock ledges to gain a V-chimney (Lamb's Chimney). Climb the chimney to its top then make a long stride and reach to the right in order to make a delicate move up to easier

The magnificent west face of Pillar Rock.

ground and a small stance in the corner. Nut belays in the steep crack above. (Originally a chimney to the left was climbed—Taylor's Chimney—with a traverse back to belay, this looks desperate!)

8. 80ft (24m), (4b). Traverse right to beneath an overhanging corner crack (Oppenheimer's Chimney). This is the crux! The footholds are small. From a good flake below the most overhanging section it is necessary to place the feet high on the right wall, whilst either jamming or laybacking, until a long reach gives a good but rickety hold enabling a pull to be made over the difficulties. Continue up a short wall to a good ledge on the shoulder. The start of the West Wall Traverse lies just up and over to the right.

Rib and Slab Climb—Summary

Start roughly in the centre of the West Face. Below a large embedded block (the start of New West Climb) scrambling leads in about 40 ft (12m) to a ledge at the back of a wide groove—the ledge being at the same height as the embedded block in the scree gully to the right.

1. 30ft (9m). Continue up grassy rocks to a ledge beneath the distinct rock rib on the right of the wide groove.

2. 55ft (17m). Move right onto the rib and climb steeply but with good holds until small ledges on the left are reached. Climb the slab above to a ledge and belays.

3. 25ft (8m), (4a). Climb into the groove above with one very hard bit to reach a good flake in the bed of the groove. Once this is reached the difficulty eases and the belay is

not far above. One very hard move.

4. 40ft (12m). Climb the fine arete on the left to a stance.

5. 70ft (21m). A magnificent pitch. Take the line of small incut holds traversing rightwards until it is possible to climb straight up the centre of the slab above. Alternatively just to the right the nose provides a spectacular line of least resistance. Both lead to a good block belay.

6. 80ft (24m). Go up right slightly then straight up the Blistered Slab on incredibly rough rock keeping left to reach to the top of Pillar Rock.

North-West Climb and Rib and Slab Climb—Description

As you raise your eyes above the pines of Ennerdale and see it towering massively above the steep hillside there is no doubting the grandeur of this mountain crag. The crag is Pillar Rock—the most elegant and aesthetic climbing cliff in England. Virtually a thousand-foot tower, detached and separate at its summit from Pillar Mountain behind, its complex walls of rock yield some super climbs. In truth an attempt to select a few routes from this crag is spoilt by choice. But an attempt must be made and the two climbs described and linked here provide some of the most memorable and distinctive mountain rock climbing to be had anywhere. Placed here, taking the challenge of Low Man then traversing across to scale the 300ft (91m) of perfection that is the west face, finally to finish on the very summit, their pedigree is flawless.

In describing the rock two locals' comments stand out more than the rest. Wordsworth in his poem 'The Brothers' wrote:

> You see yon precipice; it wears the shape
> Of a vast building made of many crags;
> And in the midst is one particular rock
> That rises like a column from the vale,
> Whence by our shepherds it is called the Pillar.[1]

The other comment was made by a local shepherd and recorded as follows by one of Lakeland's greatest rock climbing pioneers and the first guidebook writer to Pillar Rock—H. M. Kelly:

'Finally, one must recall the extraordinary demonstration of interest in Pillar Rock shown by both climbers and the general public on Easter Sunday, April 4th, 1926, a century after the first ascent. It is hardly an exaggeration to say that there were scores of climbers and non-climbers who

Susan Lund on the ârete, pitch 4, of Rib and Slab.

reached its top by devious routes, whilst on the fellside ledges, above and on both sides of the Rock, were large numbers of lookers-on perched like so many sea-birds on their cliffs. The culminating moment of the day occurred, for me, as I reached the scree on the west side after descending the New West. It carried me back to the days of veneration and awe, for before me stood a very elderly farmer and his wife gazing up at the great sweep of cliff before them. "Ay, it's a Grand Staein," he said simply. A sentiment, surely, that has echoed time and again in many a cragsman's heart.'[2]

An inspiration to any mountain crag climber, Pillar is a rock so perfect in form as to be regarded by its devotees as nothing less than divine. In the days when a good walk was an integral part of the rock climbing day experienced climbers were often asked what they thought of Pillar. If their response did not include the best on Pillar, despite any achievements elsewhere, they could never be taken seriously. It is with some reverence then that you, as an aspiring Lakeland climber, should pay due homage to the Pillar Rock.

I am tempted to report that the July day we set forth from Gatesgarth in Buttermere to climb the North-West and Rib and Slab on Pillar was the only fine day during the whole of the summer of 1987. It wasn't, of course, but I think it is fair to say it was the most perfect. Despite the early hour of departure the sun shone from a sky of pure blue. Yet its heat was not to be appreciated until contrasted with the cool shade as we passed into the dark conifers. Only then did we miss its warmth on our backs.

I know these woods are often referred to in disparaging terms—with expressions like 'ugly ranked rows of conifers'. But today, entering into their complete darkness with only the occasional shaft of brilliant sunlight penetrating the canopy, with all the ground, excepting the slate grey path, smooth chocolate brown from the litter of needles, and with the wonderful natural pine smell of the resin generated by a sun that was later to be hot enough to crack the rocks, it was impossible to feel any animosity.

When you hop the stile and emerge onto open fellside after the first plantation you look directly across to majestic Pillar. The siren calls. Even the crystal clear waters of the Lisa cannot hold back your headlong dash to the fabled rock.

The first route is a masterpiece of both route finding and climbing interest—Botterill's other great climb. It gains in

PILLAR ROCK – WEST FACE

Abseil Descent

Crux Chimney

Crux Groove

WEST COVE GULLY

West Wall Traverse (Descent from Low Man)

NEW WEST CLIMB

RIB & SLAB CLIMB

belay point

Pillar West face showing Rib and Slab and New West route.

strength and as the exposure increases (you start from a ledge that is already some 300ft (91m) above the ground) so too does the technical interest. The final bastion of rock, after some 200ft (61m) of climbing, takes the line of least resistance. There are no ready escapes onto easier ground and from below the line looks highly improbable. It is most bold in concept and the difficulties are sustained until the final crux pitch.

The route, particularly in the upper reaches, is most modern in concept. The very scale of it means it is a serious undertaking

Susan Lund on the edge of the wall, pitch 6.

in his book *The Complete Mountaineer* confirms the shattering effect it had on the scene of the day:

'The success of a party led by Mr. F. W. Botterill up the north-west side of the famous rock in 1906 demands attention as a remarkable performance, but the route is much too difficult to become either useful or popular. This and the direct ascent of Scafell Pinnacle should be classed as *sui generis*. They are not justifiable without careful exploration and preparation. The latter might well include a strong gymnasium net fixed below the steepest portion.'[3]

Thinking back on the route you can't fail to recall the overall impression of purpose and exposure. From the start you feel, rightly, that there is going to be no compromise of either. Below the Green Ledge there is already 300ft (91m) of space and above, some 400ft (122m) of unbroken blackness until the first sunshine can be enjoyed on the shoulder of High Man. The individual moves and technicalities will be recalled time and again: this is where a route rises from being one which takes an inspiring line to one that is also a great climb.

Vivid pictures of situations, moves and emotions will readily flood back to all who climb this route. Without effort the 405ft (123m) collage will break into individual moment. Recalling the first awkward chimney, then the sudden delicate contrast of the Three Step Traverse; the corner chimney that requires the positive appproach and the skill to handjam, the feeling of commitment when this is climbed and nothing but space can be seen below; the comfort of the big ledge countered by the frowning rock above; the thin moves to reach Le Coin followed by the reality of the vertical wall to be climbed out of the recess; the precariously committing move to reach the detached block that forms the Block Ledge; the sheer technical involvement of Lamb's Chimney, with the glance across left to the line of the original ascent—Taylor's Chimney—thinking 'My God did they climb *that*?' Then finally the overhanging corner of Oppenheimer's Chimney —the last straw? No there is a hold. It's loose! Then the comfort and sunshine on the big shoulder of Low Man.

Moving across the West Wall Traverse takes you into a different world. From early afternoon the west face gets the sunshine full on and it is without doubt the most attractive wall of rock on Pillar. Ever since I can remember I've had a hand-coloured Mayson's black and white photograph of the West Face of Pillar Rock hanging on my wall. As a child,

and the line above is in no way obvious until you commit youself to climb it. It is undoubtedly an extraordinary climb for its day and in many respects Fred Botterill's greatest new route. Despite the names of the other ascenionists associated with various parts of the route, he led it in its entirety. At that time to have had the skill and audacity to succeed on such a route using hemp rope and bendy boots is the mark of climbing genius.

Today it is hard to grasp the fact that this route was climbed as early as 1906 but a contemporary comment by George Abraham

its sun-reddened slabs and ribs, its black grooves, the tiny pinpricks that represented 'rock climbers' on its summit, with Jordan Gully on one side and a white cloud-studded blue space on the other this mighty sweeping rock stood independent and erect, epitomising everything that was challenging, awe-inspiring, exciting and beautiful. I yearned to climb it.

Even those of you with a romantic impression of Pillar, will suffer no disappointment should you climb Rib and Slab on a sunny day. It has been described as one of the best climbs on the rock. With a pedigree such as this it is unneccessary to detail the route microscopically—needless to say the quality of the climbing and the position are quite exceptional.

The open and bold nature of the climbing is adequately balanced by the excellence of the holds and the climbing is remarkably consistent. More a technical balance climb than one of great strenuousness, there is one section that provides the exception to the rule, adding to the fascination of the climb. This is the very awkward move to gain the groove on pitch three (actually by-passed to the right by Holland on the first ascent but ascended by the others in the party with a rope from above). Any more moves of this standard would qualify the route for, at least, a Very Severe grade. This would be a pity for the difficulties are short and anyone in real difficulty would most probably flick a sling and lasso the good flake, tantalisingly out of reach, in the bed of the groove!

It is pitch three, as described here with its exposed traverse onto a sweeping wall of unbroken rock hanging high on the West Face, that provides one of the most aesthetic and intrinsically interesting sections of climbing to grace any climb. If this single pitch were singled out from the rest of the 300ft (91m) of climbing and placed on a 70ft (21m) lowly crag it would still produce something outstanding.

I have always loved the popular description of the top pitch—climb the blistered slab. Its execution fully lives up to the provocative image. Is this the roughest piece of volcanic rock in England? Holland wrote of his first ascent:

'From the belay we kept to the New West for a few feet and then stepped across to the left on slabs of most marvellous rock, sound as a bell and almost incredibly rough. Gabbro itself is scarcely more destructive to finger tips and rubber soles.'[4]

Finally, exalted, breathless, full of reverence, you pull onto the top of Pillar, the rock of rocks.

The bonus after a full day on Pillar is that the return to Gatesgarth involves two descents with only one ascent! We returned tired of limb yet content to make the final drop from Scarth Gap as the stars began to appear. Below, Buttermere was so faultlessly reflective black that it appeared as a large gaping hole in the valley floor. Fleetwith Pike was bathed in pure butter yellow, a colour so intense that brackens burned electric green and the rocks fire red. Later passing sleeping Derwentwater the sky graduated from black-blue to orange in the west and the banded chromatographic reflection was one of silver through to crimson. The end of a perfect summer's climbing day on Pillar Rock—could anyone ask for more?

1. 1800—'The Brothers' by W. Wordsworth.
2. 1934 Guidebook published by the Fell & Rock climbing Club—*Pillar* by H. M. Kelly.
3. 1907 Methuen & Co. Ltd. —*The Complete Mountaineer* by George Abraham.
4. 1919 *Journal of the Fell & Rock Climbing Club*—'New Climbs in Wasdale' by C. F. Holland.

PILLAR ROCK: New West Climb

NEW WEST CLIMB: 290ft (88m), Difficult.
First Ascent: George and Ashley Abraham, C. W. Barton, J. H. Winger, 26 May 1901.
Location: West Face of High Man, Pillar Rock.
Attitude: Faces west.
Access: If it is intended to climb only on the West Face then one ascends up into West Cove Gully from the right end of the Green Ledge. A slight ascent is made and then a short descent into the stream bed itself (you are now in the middle of West Waterfall). Climb up the other, right, side to follow up the path winding up the rocks to the scree of West Cove Gully. The West Face lies directly above.
Descent: As for Rib and Slab Climb.

Al Phizacklea swings round the edge after the desperate crux chimney on pitch 4 of the New West route.

New West Climb—Summary

Start directly above a large flake embedded in the scree approximately 40ft (12m) below the deep gully (West Jordan Gully) on the right side of the face.

1. 70ft (21m). Climb up diagonally left then follow a rib up to a small corner. Continue up the stairs to a good ledge.

2. 35ft (11m). A chimney groove leads to a small ledge. Move over left to a better belay.

3. 55ft (17m). Up the steep groove and slab until steeper rocks above force a step down and short traverse left to the foot of the steep obvious chimney rift. Awkward place to stand but good nut belays.

4. 60ft (18m). Climb the chimney (the distinct and desperate crux when wet) until after about 30ft (9m) it is possible to step delicately out right to the rib (make sure you are high enough here). From the edge of the rib move across right until a large detached block can be used to reach up and gain a ledge and belay.

5. 40ft (12m). Move up to the right to a ledge at the upper right corner. High belay.

6. 30ft (9m). A little scoop leads to the top of High Man—the summit of Pillar Rock.

New West Climb—Description

The Abraham Brothers, George and Ashley, are inextricably linked with the early years of rock climbing; their pioneering exploits, books and—most of all—wonderful photography have left an indelible image of adventurous fun. In the Lakes today they have a kind of fan following; it's called the. Abraham Club. This is a club with a difference; for there are no officials, no rules, no paperwork, no AGMs—its members simply embrace the free climbing spirit epitomised by the brothers from Keswick. Ashley himself became the first President of the Fell and Rock Climbing Club of the English Lake District and his words recorded at their first annual dinner set the mood:

'To me the steep chimney, the hard struggle up a vertical crack, the delicate balancing round an overhanging nose with a drop beneath one—as Kipling graphically puts it, "as straight as a beggar can spit" —are still amongst the best things this world affords. At present it is the rocks that fascinate, and any slight justification I have for standing here in my capacity tonight lies in the fact that I am a rock climber and lover of our Lakeland fells first, and a mountaineer afterwards.'[1]

Rain again: masssed clouds, weeping and dripping crags. Ambleside in August. Threatened with yet another session on the boring wall, choking on chalk, sweating with the masses, blinking gaudy coloured tights I shuddered involuntarily. Then there was Al Phizacklea: 'Pillar and the New West, get a rope, lets go.' The real clouds remained unbroken but metaphorically the sun shone brilliantly. We picked up two more cragsmen en route, the irrepressible Tony Greenbank and the teetotal landlord of the famous Golden Rule, John Lockley.

We made rapidly for the truculent clouds plucking at the heights of Scarth Gap. From here, lusting for action, our half-run-half-walk turned into a full-speed dash to the bridge over the Lisa. Despite the pace Tony's commentary never ceased. 'Watson leads from Prost, no he's spun he's off the track, looks serious. Could be a burst tyre. No he's away again—wow man—fantastic.'

Al Phizacklea bridging the slippery groove on the New West route.

The pace slowed as we entered the shroud of clouds and drizzle that completely masked Pillar. Then when we touched the rock and felt the slime, we shuddered, soaking, waiting for the back marker to arrive, slowed by a malfunctioning knee joint. A few nagging thoughts about the actual climb began to niggle somewhere in the more rational regions of the brain.

Pillar is both big and complex—reasonably serious in poor conditions. Nailed boots would have been the best footwear in which to tackle these super-slippery rocks. But Al and I couldn't voice any reservations, not with these two veterans. The hard man rules made it imperative that they should crack first. They didn't. We found ourselves beneath the climb, somewhere 'twixt the green dripping rocks and the depthless, grey rolling mists in a surreal world of echoes and silence.

'Is this right?' I asked as I struggled up a steep stairway of insecurity. 'Yeah sure, come on man, if I had a pound for every time I've been here I'd be a rich man.' I just knew it was too hard—I couldn't deal with it under the prevailing conditions. As I made the mental decision to retreat Tony beamed in again. 'What you doing man? You're on the wrong bit of rock,' and, with increasing alacrity, 'Come on Bill get on route man—you're just wasting time—it's up here, here.' He stood higher up the West Cove precipitous scree, wagging an admonishing finger at what was patently a staircase compared with what I was on. 'Thanks Tony,' I said knowingly.

First I took the lead then Al. We fought our way up what was a very demanding struggle. Then came a right-angled groove which Al led authoritatively, his long legs bridged far, and which I thought was about as hard as I wanted to manage under such conditions. Then I had to go up and step left onto a little smooth bottomless slab which led to a hostile-looking steep chimney. To prevent rope drag I took an intermediate belay, brought Al across, then set off again.

Somebody rattled the cage, for Tony started expounding again with increased excitement: 'This is it man, wow I wish I had a pound for every time I've been here. Listen, listen carefully here man, hey are you listening? Don't go too high. You make a delicate move out onto the right rib, there are no handholds to balance out but once you reach it you will know you are in the right place.'

'Tony,' I said, 'there is no way you can move out here and stand on that rib, it's totally smooth.'

'Hey man don't go too low—come on man, don't go too low, whats wrong with you.' Despite my predicament, jamming up a smooth and insecure dark space with only grease for comfort I couldn't help hooting with laughter. Tony is just so totally Tony; enlivening on any and every occasion.

There was a time in that chimney when I honestly felt I couldn't get any higher. Written in code in the Fell and Rock Climbing Club guide is the fact that it is desperate when wet and greasy—'Quickly becomes very difficult in bad conditions'! Then a high step, lifting foot with hand, enabled me just to get my boot on a little edge and I crimped up and up and up to something. Then came the worn step traverse on the right rib. 'That's it,' Tony yelled accurately, 'Fantastic man, fantastic—I wish I had a pound for. . . .' etc.

It really is a tremendous route, taking a natural passage up through what on that day we could only imagine to be impressive rock scenery. As Al wound his way up the top pitch Tony pointed elsewhere but with singular common sense and devotion to the rock in front Al took the line to the summit cairn undaunted. Inevitably we chorused to Tony, 'I wish we had a pound for every time you've been here.' Grinning he trumped by pulling out his flask of steaming tea and pouring the life-saving fluid.

It's a natural passage up a great piece of rock as much a classic as is Beethoven's fifth. If you do tackle it in the wet, when the mists roll, remember you are on a big mountain crag and the climbing can be very hard under slippery conditions. George Abraham proudly stated it was his favourite climb—sanctification enough for any rock climber.

1. 1975 Heineman—*Camera On The Crags* by Alan Hankinson.

V-Groove

The Black Wall

SINISTER
GROOVES

belay point

HONISTER
WALL

BUTTERMERE—BUCKSTONE HOW

BUCKSTONE HOW: Honister Wall, Sinister Grooves.
Map Ref: NY 223143.
Guidebooks: *Rock Climbing in the Lake District* by Birkett, Cram Eilbeck and Roper. *Buttermere and Eastern Crags* (FRCC Guide) by D. Craig and R. Graham.
Attitude: Faces south-west.
Altitude: 1200ft (370m).
Rock: Slate (generally sound but caution should be exercised).
Access: From the summit of Honister Pass, which divides Buttermere from Borrowdale (car park behind the youth hostel), take the old quarry track directly above the youth hostel. This ends in slate scree which should be crossed. Keep low to gain the right-hand end of the crag (10 minutes).

Descent: Traverse right to descend a rake which is actually the top edge of the crag. *Great care* must be taken to avoid knocking loose slate onto anyone below.

Observations: Originally named Yew Crags this piece of rock gives excellent climbing in an imposing situation high above the Buttermere side of Honister Pass. Bill Peascod first explored the potential here and he frequently returned to reascend Honister Wall—his favourite climb.

Descent: Traverse right to descend a rake which is actually the top edge of the crag. Great care must be taken to avoid knocking loose slate onto anyone below.

Buttermere How showing Honister Wall and Sinister Grooves routes.

BUCKSTONE HOW: Honister Wall and Sinister Grooves

Looking into Birkness Combe with High Crag on the left edge of the basin, with Eagle Crag and Grey Crags to the right.

HONISTER WALL: 285ft (87m), Hard Severe.
First Ascent: W. Peascod, S. B. Beck, 19 May 1946.
SINISTER GROOVES: 250ft (76m), Very Severe (4c).
First Ascent: W. Peascod, S. B. Beck, 31 March 1946.
Location: Buckstone How (Yew Crags on the OS map), Honister Pass, Buttermere.

Honister Wall—Summary

Roughly in the centre of the crag there is a very large block in the path at the foot of the rock. The route starts up the clean wall immediately to the right of this block.

1. 60ft (18m). Climb the wall from the ground (stepping off the block misses out some worthwhile climbing) with moves right at the hard bits to arrive at a perch and shattered block belay.

2. 85ft (26m). Move across the exposed corner to the left to gain the airy arete. Climb this to a a short corner and pull onto the wall above to continue directly to a commodious ledge and large flake belay on its left end.

3. 40ft (12m). The Black Wall. The object is the clean wall to the right and crossing this constitutes the crux. Climb the corner to a good runner (excellent Friend 1) then traverse delicately rightwards across the wall to gain the far rib. Climb the rib to a belay on the right.

4. 60ft (18m). Climb diagonally leftwards to cross underneath a small overhang. Then move across diagonally rightwards, above the overhang, to a short steep wall which requires a final bold pull to reach the top.

Sinister Grooves—Summary

This starts some 30ft (9m) left of the large block and the start of Honister Wall. The most distinctive feature, the second pitch, is a deep V-groove about 80ft (24m) above the ground.

1. 80ft (24m). Climb the wall to gain a

Moving into the corner on the 2nd pitch of Honister Wall.

shallow groove. This becomes increasingly awkward as you climb to a stance.

2. 80ft (24m). The groove is climbed until a small rock ledge can be gained on the left. From this go straight up, climbing a rib (some loose rock) to a large vegetated ledge. Across the ledge is a thin crack leading into the large and obvious chimney crack.

3. 90ft (27m). The crack to enter the chimney proves steeper and harder than at first appears. But once the chimney is entered the climbing becomes more straightforward and leads to the top of the crag.

Honister Wall and Sinister Grooves—Description

There are two important qualities of Buckstone How that are worth noting: its accessibility, ten minutes' easy walk from the car, and its quick-drying nature. Being slate rock, with an almost quarried appearance, it repels the water and its smooth character means that any precipitated moisture is soon dispersed. It is therefore a good venue for a short day, perhaps when the morning has been wet but the day improves in the afternoon. Early spring, and even the occasional sunny winter day, has given me many an excellent afternoon's activity high on Buckstone How.

Despite the rather ramshackle appearance of the place, the climbing is a good deal more interesting and exposed than first impressions would suggest. Although the crag is a natural face of rock it is surrounded on all sides by slate workings. They lie at its foot, pour over its top and sweep down the gullies on either side. Across the dramatic sweep of Honister Pass there are even more workings which all add to the special rather impressive atmosphere. Of course the slate rock does demand care and, although generally good, requires considerate use at all times.

Bill Peascod frequently reclimbed Honister Wall on his return from Australia. It became his party piece, and he introduced more than his fair share of young ladies to the joys of rock climbing on this route. Funnily enough I tasted its delights only when I had climbed all the other routes on the crag and it was only then that realised I had missed out on a really excellent climb of the grade.

Hard Severe always seems to give a distinguished climb; something that isn't quite Very

Susan Lund on the edge of Black Wall of Honister Wall.

Severe but makes for a demanding and sustained lead that is markedly harder than Severe. I should have known that Bill was onto something good, but from below Honister Wall holds little promise of excitement; it appears to be one of those rather loose routes that ramble up a crag without any real distinction. Nothing could be further from reality. In fact the climb offers line, exposure and technical interest.

The starting wall fortunately just falls short of being very hard by virtue of the fact that it naturally allows you to step right each time the direct line runs out of holds. What looked like an easy stroll from below turns out to be a very interesting lead and takes you to a belay where the full effects of the steep ground plunging away to the tiny road far beneath are further compounded by the sparseness of the stance. From here the climbing involves constant exposure, reaching a crescendo when the corner is successfully traversed to gain the knife-edged crest of the hanging arete.

Above this, a comfortable ledge must be quitted to gain the precarious and delicate Black Wall. This is the crux and requires both the bold and the nimble approach—it is essential to get your footwork right here. It always seems mentally more demanding to switch on to climbing something reasonably difficult and exposed when you are moving away from the safety of a good stance, out into the unknown. So it is here.

The last eighty-foot pitch, requiring prudent ropework if it is to be run into one, remains interesting with the very last move as delightful as any other on the whole route. All routes should end thus! When it is done a traverse rightwards leads to a natural rake which slants down, then across, to the far end of the crag. But do not make the mistake of dropping too far down too early, as this leads into the clean groove which plunges down the right end of the crag—this is Groove Two, VS.

Sinister Grooves is a mite more technical than Honister Wall and gives some unique climbing. I first climbed it with the irrepressible Ray McHaffie on a rather indifferent day. We were both somewhat slowed by the damp weeping from the groove on the second pitch, since it had been raining hard earlier in the day, but this is the exception rather than the rule—generally the climb takes little drainage. The next time I was with Bill Peascod on a late autumn afternoon, a bitter wind numbed the fingers and fluttered the occasional flake of snow past our shivering vision. Despite my cold hands and lack of feeling therein, the route gave me immense pleasure.

The route has a most distinct character, winding its way up the tallest section of the crag. It's full of surprises and although you usually cannot see the next pitch, or the logic of the whole line, from any single position whilst climbing it, in execution it naturally flows together. Whilst the main inspiration of the first pitch was undoubtedly to reach the formidable-looking corner groove some 80ft (24m) above the ground it transpires that it is itself no pushover. The first groove, above an easy wall, proves markedly more awkward the higher you get.

The corner groove has a crack in its back and a smooth hanging slab, shaped not unlike an elongated earlobe, forming its left wall, which proves exciting however you tackle it. Some squeeze into it and handjam the crack whilst others bridge wide and use the tiny holds available mainly on its left side. Whatever the technique employed it is the top few feet that are the most precarious and demand the most concentration. I remember taking an alternative belay just above the groove, watching Bill with interest to see how he would fare on it. He was impressive, utilising the tiny incuts and rugosities on the left wall, standing up on them with total confidence. So nonchalant was his style that a casual observer, on the ground below, could have been forgiven for imagining them to be like brick tops in size and but, as you will see, they are most distinctly not.

When reached, the natural amphitheatre above presents an easily identifiable and straightforward-looking escape route. The stark chimney looks meaningfully poised but the simple-looking crack to reach it will be mentally dismissed by most. It proves to be rather more absorbing than it would first appear!

Both routes have a great deal of character, offering climbing that is unique to Buckstone How. Despite the quarry workings and obvious presence of man's past industry it feels a good place to be. And if you find yourself there during a moody afternoon when the black monopoly of Fleetwith Pike and the pass below are only broken by a silver thread winding its way to Buttermere, the green light at the end of this tunnel valley, then so much the better.

Below Buckstone How and Fleetwith Pike the silver thread winds its way down Honister to Buttermere.

BUTTERMERE—HIGH CRAG

HIGH CRAG: The Philistine.
Map Ref: NY 183145.
Attitude: Faces east.
Altitude: 1500ft (460m).
Rock: Clean Rhyolite.
Access: Follow the track from Gatesgarth up to Scarth Gap. The crag lies on the open fellside some way above the track and is best reached by first passing through a gate and then following the fence and wall line steeply up until steep scree leads directly to the crag (25 minutes).
Descent: Take a line well over to the left.
Observations: A clean and attractive crag placed high on the fellside above Gatesgarth.

HIGH CRAG: The Philistine

THE PHILISTINE: 175ft (53m), E1 (5b).
First Ascent: E. Cleasby, B. Birkett, 22 June 1975.
Location: High Crag, Buttermere.

The Philistine—Summary

In the morning the sun catches the north-east (right) wall of High Crag. The twin caves, known as the Goblin's Eyes, make it readily identifiable. In any case the blunt clean arete left of the eyes, in the centre of the crag, is the main feature and this is the line of the climb. Start at a ledge below the left side of the arete.

1. 125ft (38m), (5b). Climb the wall to the overhang and step round to the right to gain a thin crack. Go up this until moves can be made delicately left to gain the arete. Continue directly up this to belay.

2. 50ft (15m). Easier rocks finish the climb.

The Philistine—Description

In many ways the clean sweeping lines and the obviously steep nature of High Crag make it the most appealing piece of rock for high-standard climbing in Buttermere. Its initial appearance is no deception, and despite its brevity there are some excellent routes to be climbed here. I hope you will forgive my self-indulgence when I say that one of the best routes of the E1 grade hereabouts is that following the bold central arete named the Philistine.

When Ed Cleasby and I set off for High Crag one glorious June day we were both extremely fit and confident enough to tackle anything. It was our first visit to the cliff and we were immediately struck by the magnificent clean arete which, after reference to our updated guide appeared to be unclimbed. I think the guide was borrowed from Mike Lynch, who religiously updated his guidebooks with new route information. Apart from handwritten notes, he also stuck in magazine information and typed route descriptions making for a guide that was literally bulging with the latest information. We just couldn't believe our luck.

Ed and I had a system designed to share the leads reasonably fairly. We used to alternate and that day it was Ed's turn for the first lead. We discussed the route and agreed to try it on sight (abseil inspection being at that time somewhat foreign to the Lakeland new routing ethic); but first it was agreed that we would warm up on Samson—a route taking the wall to the left of the arete. In effect, the easy pitches didn't count in our system, it was one pitch and this meant I would then get to lead that superb-looking arete.

Mysteriously Ed failed on Samson, a route well within his capabilities, and I ended up leading it. This meant, of course, that Ed got to lead the plumb magnificent line of the Philistine. Only a country boy at heart, I wised up to the big world shortly after this. At least I suggested the route name first, and it

The Philistine on High Crag.

Top:
Bob Wightman high on the ârete of
The Philistine with Buttermere below.

Above:
Al Phizacklea moving right beneath
the roof on The Philistine to find the
thin crack.

Above right:
Al Phizacklea in the thin crack that
provides entry to the fine bold ârete
on The Philistine.

does seem quite appropriate when you know a little of the background history.

The climbing itself is on excellent rock and very open in nature. It is by no means over-protected, and a cool approach is necessary, but protection does materialise when needed most. It's one of those elegant routes that appears striking without being overbearing and whilst requiring a degree of boldness, its execution is agreeably reasonable for the grade. One word of advice; work out who leads the night before—on arrival you'll both want to do it.

EAGLE GRAG
BIRKNESS COMBE

Nail Ledge

Green Ledge

Little Botterills

EAGLE FRONT

belay point

Eagle Crag showing Eagle Front.

BUTTERMERE—EAGLE CRAG

EAGLE CRAG: Eagle Front.
Map Ref: NY 172145.
Guidebooks: *Rock Climbing in the Lake District* Birkett, Cram, Eilbeck and Roper. *Buttermere and Eastern Crags* (FRCC Guide) by D. Craig and R. Graham.
Attitude: faces north.
Altitude: 1,750ft (530m).
Rock: Rhyolite—apparently vegetated and dank but actually good and clean.
Access: The track from Gatesgarth farm leads across level fields and up towards Scarth Gap until, at an elbow in the track, a distinct path breaks off rightwards. Follow this up into the basin to rise steeply again to the centre of Eagle Crag—the bastion which dominates the upper left wall (1 hour).
Descent: Skirt well over to the right until a path weaves down the right side of a steep scree-filled gully.
Observations: The major crag of the area.

EAGLE CRAG: Eagle Front

EAGLE FRONT: 490ft (149m), Very Severe (4c).
First Ascent: Bill Peascod, Bert Beck, 23 June 1940.
Location: Eagle Crag, Birkness Combe, Buttermere.

Bob Wightman high on the striking corner crack of the last pitch on Eagle Crag.

Eagle Front—Summary

Start about 60ft (18m) left of the point where the nose of the crag first nudges the scree.

1. 60ft (18m). Pleasantly up the rib and move right to a recess and belay.

2. 90ft (27m), 4c. Climb the steep groove moving right when possible to the foot of a leftward-sloping gangway—Little Botterill's. Follow this to a steep shallow groove. Climb this to a small ledge and move right to another ledge. Go left across awkward sloping slabs then follow a line of flake handholds leading to a ledge up on the right.

3. 60ft (18m), 4c. Gain a shallow groove from the right end of the ledge with a hard pull to start—Headstand Move. But then a step right gains easier ground which continues to reach the long ledge—Grass Terrace.

4. 75ft (23m) (Grass Terrace). Traverse easily along left to cross a mossy slab to a rock ledge.

5. 45ft (14m), (4c). From the higher ledge climb the steep wall until delicate moves enable a groove on the right to be gained. Continue up this to a sloping stance—Nail Ledge.

6. 65ft (20m), (4b). Make an exposed traverse right, crossing several ribs, to a waterworn slab. Move up this to a stance below the striking corner crack.

7. 60ft (18m), (4b). Climb it until a step out right gives a stance with a view—the Crack.

8. 35ft (11m). Easy ground to the top.

Eagle Front—Description

Of all the Lakeland valleys Buttermere in many ways remains the most unspoilt and idyllic. Her waters are the greenest, her lands the quietest. Maureen Richardson at Gatesgarth Farm still welcomes into her back parlour the local climbers to recall, over a cup of tea which inevitably stretches to a minimum of three, the antics of Bill Peascod and the old West Cumberland team. It's as if time has stood still, in this valley, and it seems an infinitely more caring world because of it.

Whilst it is no longer true to say that Birkness Combe remains a forgotten sanctuary, it is it is markedly quieter than its near neighbour, Borrowdale. It is also true that the 400ft (120m) main face of Eagle Crag remains undiminished and just as dominating as it always was. The climb known as Eagle Front is still the most natural way to gain the striking corner crack positioned so compulsively at the top of the face.

Because so little of the stage for this climb has actually changed I'll let Bert Beck take over the story:

'Birkness Combe had always seemed an attractive climbing ground, and after the institution of petrol rationing, those attractions grew the greater for being near Workington. And no one can visit Birkness Combe without being impressed by the magnificent 400-foot face of Eagle Crag, of which the western and larger half was, at the beginning of summer, virgin ground. Occasionally too, it seems, my newly-made friend, William Peascod, had traced imaginary routes up it. We both concurred that so fine and sheer a face had urgent need of one or the other. . .

'On June 1 therefore our siege began in earnest. A weekend camp was pitched by the edge of the lake, a large quantity of supplies installed, and, on an exceedingly hot day, the attacking party (not without some regrets) tore themselves away from the pleasant purlieus of Buttermere and sweated their way up to the Combe.'[1]

The man himself, Bill Peascod, also recalls that June day:

'From the foot of Scarth Gap Pass the way lies up the fellside to the right, gently climbing under a knot of reddish crag, and above a steep little outcrop, surmounted by a rowan tree, which offers a splendid view of the valley below and sometimes a pleasant little waterfall. Above the waterfall outcrop and across the fell a wall is reached in time and beyond it the noticeable moraines and boulders of the extinct glacier. This is the floor of Birkness Combe.

'Once there the eye is arrested by the great mass of Eagle Crag—further up and to the left hand side of the Combe. It is a very impressive pile. At its right-hand end it presents the sharp profile of the so-called Western Buttress and to its left the deep clefts of Birkness Gully and Birkness Chimney. Cutting the centre of this great five hundred feet high face is a long, increasingly well defined crack or gully; this is Central Chimney. On this day in June 1940, the whole mass of the front of Eagle Crag, from the corner which locates the Western Buttress Route to Eastern Buttress away to the left of the main face, was totally unclimbed. It was a vast expanse of rock—big, steep, impressive. We couldn't understand why this magnificent face had never been climbed. We were to find out why in the weeks that lay ahead.'[2]

Both Bill and Bert had a great affinity for exploration. Loose, vegetated rock, if it had any effect upon them at all, actually fuelled their enthusiasm. They were not looking for the isolated delectable move, nor aiming to gain an aesthetic rib or wall of rock. Their challenge was the whole—to make a way from beginning to top—to solve the total problem and scale the entity of the face. To them a masterpiece of ascent was not the clinically sterile straight line from bottom to top but one which linked the natural features, flowing and weaving with the rock—experiencing the contrasting emotions of fear and courage and, for them, the ultimate adventure.

Remember too, that the rules were different. They had to be, for their equipment—Woolworth's rubbers, two rope slings and the strands of hemp that linked them—meant that one simply had to play the game without cheating. Bill wrote of their predicament, so equipped, high on the face at the Nail Ledge:

'Above the overhang [above the steep little rib that starts pitch 5] and short groove is probably the finest situation on the climb, a sloping stance and poor belay. The view of the Combe below is interrupted by neither rock nor grass. The walls above and to the left may be written off; only to the right does the way seem feasible, and on this ascent the traverse, across a water-worn slab on rounded holds, became increasingly "interesting" when a film of water made its presence felt on rubber-soled footgear. When one gets into such a position—the second none too happily placed, the ground a long way below, and progress in any direction only possible by movements which are attended by "natural hazards"—I think a climber must cease to regard himself as a member of a party, welded together by three strong strands of rope, and climb with the intensity and concentration of a man going solo on similar rocks.'[3]

The tongue-in-cheek comment regarding the strength of the hemp rope can really be disregarded. To all intents and purposes the pioneering effort was remarkable. A slip from either leader or second, Bill or Bert, would most probably have proved disastrous. That, then, is the scene for the climb and if you wish to experience something of the same adventure you should resist the temptation to clip the scurrilous pegs that have crept into place in a number of locations. However, even with modern equipment, there is often precious little else in the form of runner or belay and in the event prudence may be the wisest recourse—you must make your own decision.

I must admit that the overall appearance of the face, particulary if the day is damp or overcast, can look anything but inviting. I once passed it by for the more obvious sunny attractions of Grey Crag just across the way. Alas, there is some moss, and the traverse along Grass Terrace does involve an easy

Looking down on Bob Wightman high on the striking corner crack of the last pitch of Eagle Front.

stroll over grass! Still that's the nature of the climb and if you are worried about a little mud on the boots perhaps you really should go elsewhere.

Whatever your first impressions from below, in execution the rock will be found to be both cleaner and technically more demanding than you suspected. On occasions it becomes alarmingly balancey—the kind of climbing that always seems to be throwing you off, where the next obvious hold never seems to materialise into quite what you hoped. It's demanding all right and good too. In the wet, as it was when Bill reclimbed it with Chris Bonington for the film *Eagle Front*, it must be extremely hard and, despite modern gear, still a little serious.

The interest begins on the second pitch with the awkward corner slab they so aptly named Little Botterill's. At the end of its very full 90ft (27m) you arrive at the Nail Ledge; so named because on the second ascent (also by Bill, some 8 years after his first), a pit nail was hammered into the rock to effect a belay. Tony Greenbank and John Wilkinson removed it, not before utilising a proper peg, in the summer of 1959. Reading the records, it is obvious that both Bill and Bert found the next move into a groove, only a short pull but made from full stretch, the hardest section of the entire climb. It isn't easy, and during the film this is the scene of the momentous occasion when Bill actually stood on Chris Bonington's head. It brought the house down when first shown, at the 1985 Kendal Film Festival. For me it showed the true grit of both of them—Bill by this time was no lightweight!

Despite the fact that the crack is a lot easier than appearances suggest from the ground far below, it is still an impressive place to be and does have a degree of technical interest. I will never forget the image of Bill working his way up the final crack, in soaking wet conditions, and exclaiming about the rogue peg in the hairline crack on the right wall. As it was there Chris suggested he might as well clip it but Bill simply said, 'I don't think I will.' He didn't! If one isolated incident can show the mettle of a man then this was indicative of Bill's free spirit.

I think in this instance it is only proper to quote again from the twenty-year-old coal miner who found himself at home in steep places:

'The final crack looks most spectacular from the floor of the Combe. To my indescribable delight it was loaded with splendid hidden handholds. Up without pause, with song in my heart, if not in my throat. A short scramble led to the top of the crag where Bert, afterwards, joined me. We sat there, together, in the sun. The evening was still; we were completely alone in the Combe—in the world! The War, the pit . . . they didn't exist. We didn't say much. What was there to say? Each of us was drenched in his own emotions, dreaming their own dreams and experiencing that most exquisite of sensations—the elation of success at having climbed something really worthwhile. We called the climb Eagle Front.'[2]

1. 1941 *Journal of the Fell and Rock climbing Club*—'A Summer Siege At Buttermere' by S. B. Beck.
2. 1985, Cicerone Press—*Journey After Dawn* by Bill Peascod.
3. 1950 *Journal of the Fell and Rock Climbing Club*—'The Cinderella of Climbing Valleys' by Bill Peascod.

BUTTERMERE—GREY CRAG

GREY CRAG: Fortiter/Dexter Wall (Combination).
Map Ref: NY 172148.
Attitude: Faces south-east.
Altitude: 2,250ft (685m).
Rock: Rhyolite, hard and rough.
Access: Take the track from Gatesgarth which leads across level fields and up as for Scarth Gap until, at an elbow in the track, a distinct path breaks off rightwards. Follow this into the basin of Birkness Combe. Grey Crag lies at the top right, High Stile, side of the Combe (1.25 hours).

Descent: It is probably best to descend to the left of Dexter Wall and then to cross underneath the wall itself and continue down to the right of Fortiter.
Observations: Grey Crag is actually composed of a number of separate rock walls and buttresses. Its nature contrasts sharply with the often dark and dank cliff of Eagle Crag in the combe below. It is therefore a sensible alternative if the latter proves to be wet or out of condition.

GREY CRAGS

Grey Crag showing Fortiter and Dexter Wall routes.

GREY CRAG: Fortiter/Dexter Wall (Combination)

FORTITER: 145ft (44m), Mild Very Severe (4b).
First Ascent: W. Peascod, S. B. Beck, 12 July 1941.
DEXTER WALL: 125ft (38m), Hard Very Severe (5a).
First Ascent: W. Peascod, S. B. Beck, 16 March 1941.
Location: Grey Crag, Birkness Combe, High Stile Face, Buttermere.

Fortiter—Summary

If one imagines the cluster that make up Grey Crag to be roughly triangular in shape then Fortiter climbs the little buttress that forms the bottom right side. Dexter Wall forms the apex of this triangle.

Start below a well-defined groove on the right of the buttress. The first objective is the rock ledge at 20ft (6m).

1. 20ft (6m). Up to the right side of the ledge.

2. 70ft (21m), (4b). Move up into the crack and climb directly to the overhang. Pull over it

to regain the crack above. Continue to a narrow rock ledge and natural flake belay.

3. 55ft (17m). Climb the corner to a ledge and continue via the arete to the top.

Dexter Wall—Summary

From the top of Fortiter walk up and across to the left end of the upper wall where there is a crack just right of the arete.

1. 125ft (38m), (5a). Climb the crack trending rightwards to a niche. Step right and continue up through the little overhang. Move up the crack for a few feet then follow a delicate traverse line rightwards into the middle of the wall. Climb the thin crack in the middle of the wall directly to the top. There is a definite crux and the best runners are a little way beneath this.

Fortiter/Dexter Wall (Combination)—Description

There are two physical qualities that make

Cynthia Grindley reaching the horizontal break in the upper wall of Dexter Wall.

Cynthia Grindley belayed by Sheila Lockhart nearing the difficult upper section of the wall on Dexter Wall.

Sheila Lockhart moves up the crack to the overhang on Fortiter.

Grey Crag worthy of a visit. The rock is hard, rough and clean, the best that Buttermere can offer and, despite the altitude, they face sufficiently south to get a good dollop of sunshine. An autumn afternoon on Grey can be a most perfect experience and there are a host of excellent short climbs to choose from.

Despite the hike in the middle, across the terrace from the top of Fortiter to the bottom of Dexter Wall, this is a good and enjoyable combination of similarly graded routes. Each gives steep climbing with Fortiter being the most reasonable, but both have enough in-

terest to warrant the Very Severe grade. Although the sub-division of this grade may arguably be a matter for personal discretion I do feel Dexter Wall just warrants the prefix Hard. Consequently this is how I have descibed it. Whilst you may disagree with the grade I don't think you will find the short difficult section lacking in interest.

Despite the brevity, Fortiter rapidly takes on a good deal of exposure. Most climbers still tend to belay on the comforting natural rock ledge and again above the overhang, rather than running it out in one. Above the ledge

Cynthia Grindley approaching the difficult crack on Dexter Wall.

Above the wall of Fortiter looking down into Birkness Combe and on to Gatesgarth.

the wall rears steeply and the overhang is sufficiently large to make you ponder. It is surmounted by a strenuous pull to gain the well-defined easier corner groove above. Protection is excellent and so are the holds. Nevertheless there is a good deal of excitement to be had.

As the name implies, Dexter Wall keeps on moving rightwards; never really seeming to get exposed as the adjacent ground trends upwards with the climbing. But the wall is steep and the climbing absorbing. Initially holds are good, sound incut finger holds up a distinct crack, and movement is easy. Suddenly the nature alters and you find yourself in the middle of a markedly perpendicular wall—it almost feels overhanging as the pulse quickens and fingers grip tighter. Above there is a thin crack and this, the crux, demands a bit of go. With runner placements that are not particularly satisfying the neckiness of this top section adds spice to an already interesting dish.

Why not give them a go. Both the first ascensionists would be ridiculously flattered if you climbed their two routes. They were like that.

Above the wall of Fortiter looking down into Birkness Combe and on to Gatesgarth.

TICK LIST OF CLIMBS

AREA 1: THE CONISTON FELLS

Dow Crag
- ☐ E2 (5b) Isengard/Samba Pa Ti
- ☐ VS (4c) Eliminate 'A'
- ☐ D Giant's Crawl
- ☐ D Ordinary Route 'C'

Wallowbarrow
- ☐ HS Thomas

AREA 2: WASDALE

Esk Buttress
- ☐ HS Bridge's Route
- ☐ E2 (5b) Central Pillar
- ☐ E5 (6a) The Cumbrian

The Napes
- ☐ VD Napes Needle
- ☐ MVS (4a) Eagle's Nest Ridge Direct

Kern Knotts
- ☐ MVS (4a) Kern Knotts Crack
- ☐ VS (4b) Innominate Crack
- ☐ HVS (5a) Buttonhook Route

East Buttress
- ☐ VS (4c) Mickledore Grooves
- ☐ E4 (6a/b) Lost Horizons
- ☐ HVS (4c) Great Eastern by the Yellow Slab

Scafell Crag
- ☐ VS (4c) Botterill's Slab
- ☐ HS Moss Ghyll Grooves

AREA 3: GREAT LANGDALE

Bowfell Buttress
- ☐ VD Bowfell Buttress Route

Gimmer Crag
- ☐ VD Ash Tree Slabs
- ☐ S 'D' Route
- ☐ VS (4b) Gimmer Crack
- ☐ E1 (5b) Gimmer String

Raven Crag
- ☐ D Middlefell Buttress
- ☐ HVS (5a) Pluto

Pavey Ark
- ☐ HVS (5a) Arcturus
- ☐ HVS (5a) Golden Slipper
- ☐ E2 (5b) Astra

White Ghyll
- ☐ VS (4c) Haste Not
- ☐ E2 (5c) Haste Not Direct
- ☐ MVS (4b) White Ghyll Wall

AREA 4: EASTERN FELLS

Castle Rock
- ☐ VS (4b) Zigzag
- ☐ E1 (5b) Thirlmere Eliminate

Dove Crag
- ☐ E5 (6a) Fear and Fascination

AREA 5: BORROWDALE

Falcon Crag
- ☐ HVS (5a) Illusion
- ☐ E2 (5c) The Niche
- ☐ MVS (4b) Hedera Grooves

Shepherd's Crag
- ☐ VD Little Chamonix
- ☐ HS Ardus

Greatend Crag
- ☐ E4 (6b) Nagasaki Grooves

Black Crag
- ☐ HVS (5a) The Mortician
- ☐ E3 (5c) Prana

Goat Crag
- ☐ E1 (5b) Praying Mantis
- ☐ E3 (5c) Bitter Oasis

AREA 6: BUTTERMERE

Buckstone How
- ☐ HS Honister Wall
- ☐ VS (4c) Sinister Grooves

High Crag
- ☐ E1 (5b) The Philistine

Eagle Crag
- ☐ VS (4c) Eagle Front

Grey Crag
- ☐ MVS (4b) Fortiter
- ☐ HVS (5a) Dexter wall

Pillar Rock
- ☐ MVS (4b) North-West Climb
- ☐ S (4a) Rib and Slab Climb
- ☐ D New West Climb

GRADED LIST OF ROCK CLIMBS

E5

Cumbrian (6a)   Esk Buttress
Fear and Fascination (6a)   Dove Crag

E4
Lost Horizons (6a/b)   East Buttress
Nagasaki Grooves (6b)   Greatend Crag

E3
Bitter Oasis (5c)   Goat Crag
Prana (5c)   Black Crag

E2
Astra (5b)   Pavey Ark
Central Pillar (5b)   Esk Buttress
Isengard (5b)   Dow Crag
Haste Not Direct (5c)   White Ghyll
Niche (5b)   Goat Crag
Samba Pa Ti (5b)   Dow Crag

E1
Gimmer String (5b)   Gimmer Crag
Philistine (5b)   High Crag
Praying Mantis (5b)   Goat Crag
Thirlmere Eliminate (5b)   Castle Rock

Hard Very Severe
Arcturus (5a)   Pavey Ark
Buttonhook Route (5a)   Kern Knotts
Dexter Wall (5a)   Grey Crag
Illusion (5a)   Lower Falcon Crag
Golden Slipper (5a)   Pavey Ark
Great Eastern by the Yellow Slab (4c) East Buttress
Mortician (5a)   Black Crag
Pluto (5a)   Raven Crag

Very Severe
Botterill's Slab (4c)   Scafell Crag
Eagle Front (4c)   Eagle Crag
Eliminate 'A' (4c)   Dow Crag
Gimmer Crack (4b)   Gimmer Crag
Haste Not (4c)   White Ghyll
Innominate Crack (4b)   Kern Knotts
Mickledore Grooves (4c)   East Buttress
Sinister Grooves (4c)   Buckstone How
Zigzag (4b)   Castle Rock

Mild Very Severe
Eagle's Nest Ridge Direct (4a)   The Napes
Fortiter (4b)   Grey Crag
Hedera Grooves (4b)   Lower Falcon Crag
Kern Knotts Crack (4a)   Kern Knotts
North-West Climb (4b)   Pillar Rock
White Ghyll Wall (4b)   White Ghyll

Hard Severe
Ardus   Shepherd's Crag
Bridge's Route   Esk Buttress
Honister Wall   Buckstone How
Moss Ghyll Grooves   Scafell Crag
Thomas   Wallowbarrow Crag

Severe
'D' Route   Gimmer Crag
Rib and Slab Climb (4a!)   Pillar Rock

Very Difficult
Ash Tree Slabs   Gimmer Crag
Bowfell Buttress   Bowfell Buttress
Little Chamonix   Shepherd's Crag
Napes Needle   The Napes

Difficult
Giant's Crawl   Dow Crag
Middlefell Buttress   Raven Crag
New West Climb   Pillar Rock

LIST OF FIRST ASCENTS

1886 June, **Napes Needle**, The Napes, W. P. Haskett-Smith.

1892 April 15, **Eagle's Nest Ridge Direct**, The Napes, G. A. Solly, W. C. Slingsby, G. P. Parker, W. A. Brigg.

1897 April 28, **Kern Knotts Crack**, Kern Knotts, O. G. Jones, H. C. Bowen.

1901 May 26, **New West Climb**, Pillar Rock, G. Abraham, A. Abraham, C. W. Barton, J. H. Winger.

1902 May 24, **Bowfell Buttress**, T. Shaw, G. H. Craig, G. R. West, C. Hargreaves, L. J. Oppenheimer.

1903 June 2, **Botterill's Slab**, Scafell Crag, F. W. Botterill, H. Williamson, J. E. Grant.

1904 August, **Ordinary Route 'C'**, Dow Crag, G. F. Woodhouse, A. J. Woodhouse.

1906 June 8, **North-West Climb**, Pillar Rock, F. W. Botterill, L. J. Oppenheimer, A. Botterill, J. H. Taylor.

1909 April, **Giant's Crawl**, Dow Crag, E. T. W. Addyman, D. T. Addyman, Stobart.

1911 September 24, **Middlefell Buttress**, Raven Crag, J. Laycock, S. W. Herford, A. R. Thomson.

1919 April 18, **'D' Route**, Gimmer Crag, G. S. Bower, P. R. Masson.

1919 July 29, **Rib and Slab Climb**, Pillar Rock, C. F. Holland, H. M. Kelly, C. G. Crawford.

1921 April 9, **Innominate Crack**, Kern Knotts, G. S. Bower, B. Beetham.

1921 June 20, **Ash Tree Slabs**, Gimmer Crag, G. S. Bower, A. W. Wakefield.

1923 June 17, **Eliminate 'A'**, Dow Crag, H. S. Gross, G. Basterfield.

1926 July 1, **Moss Ghyll Grooves**, Scafell Crag, H. M. Kelly, Blanche Eden-Smith, J. B. Kilshaw.

1928 May 5, **Gimmer Crack**, Gimmer Crag, A. B. Reynolds, G. G. Macphee.

1931 May, **Mickledore Grooves**, East Buttress, C. F. Kirkus, I. M. Waller, M. Pallis.

1931 August 21, **Great Eastern**, East Buttress, M. Linnell, S. H. Cross.

1932 July 10, **Bridge's Route**, Esk Buttress, A. W. Bridge, A. B. Hargreaves, M. Linnell, W. S. Dyson.

1933 September 10, **Yellow Slab**, East Buttress, M. Linnell, H. Pearson.

1934 June, **Buttonhook Route**, Kern Knotts, F. G. Balcombe, C. J. A. Cooper.

1939 April 22, **Zigzag**, Castle Rock, R. J. Birkett, C. R. Wilson, L. Muscroft.

1940 June 22, **Eagle Front**, Eagle Crag, W. Peascod, S. B. Beck.

1941 March 3, **Dexter Wall**, Grey Crag, W. Peascod, S. B. Beck.

1941 July 12, **Fortiter**, Grey Crag, W. Peascod, S. B. Beck.

1946 March 31, **Sinister Grooves**, Buckstone How, W. Peascod, S. B. Beck.

1946 May 9, **White Ghyll Wall**, White Ghyll, R. J. Birkett, L Muscroft, T. Hill.

1946 May 19, **Honister Wall**, Buckstone How, W. Peascod, S. B. Beck.

1946 May 26, **Little Chamonix**, Shepherd's Crag, B. Beetham.

1948 May 8, **Ardus**, Shepherd's Crag, V. Veevers, H. Westmorland, P. Holt.

1948 May 9, **Haste Not**, White Ghyll, R. J. Birkett, L. Muscroft.

1955 June 26, **Thomas**, Wallowbarrow Crag, W. F. Dowlen, D. Stroud.

1955 June 26, **Thirlmere Eliminate**, P. Ross, P. J. Greenwood (var).

1956 June 10, **Illusion**, P. Lockey, P. Ross (alt).

1956 August 10, **Hedera Grooves**, Lower Falcon Crag, P. Lockey, P. Ross (alt).

1958 July 19, **Golden Slipper**, Pavey Ark, J. A. Austin, R. B. Evans.

1958, **Pluto**—Pitch 1, Raven Crag, A. L. Atkinson. Pitch 2—P. Woods 1953. Pitch 3—E. Metcalf, J. Ramsden 1957.

1960 May 27, **Astra**, Pavey Ark, J. A. Austin, E. Metcalf (alt), D. G. Roberts.

1962 April, **Isengard**, Dow Crag, L. Brown, R. McHardy.

1962 June 17, **Central Pillar**, Esk Buttress, P. Crew, M. Owen.

1962 August 20, **The Niche**, Lower Falcon Crag, A. Liddell, R. McHaffie.

1963 April 28, **Arcturus**, Pavey Ark, J. A. Austin, E. Metcalf (var).

1963 July 15, **Gimmer String**, Pavey Ark, J. A. Austin, E. Metcalf, D. Millar (G. Cram had done it but with a right-hand finish prior to this).

1965 May 30, **Praying Mantis**, Goat Crag, L. Brown, J. S. Bradshaw.

1969 August 7, **The Mortician**, Black Crag, B. Thompson, W. A. Barnes (alt).

1971 May 2, **Haste Not Direct**, White Ghyll, J. A. Austin, R. Valentine.

1972 July 24, **Nagasaki Grooves**, Greatend Crag, C. Read, J. Adams. Free—P. Livesey 1974.

1974 May 5, **The Cumbrian**, Esk Buttress, R. Valentine, P. Braithwaite (alt). Free—M. Berzins 1977.

1974 May 12, **Bitter Oasis**, Goat Crag, P. Livesey, J. Sheard.

1975 June 22, **The Philistine**, High Crag, E. Cleasby, B. Birkett.

1976 September, **Lost Horizons**, East Buttress, P. Livesey, J. Lawrence. Free—R. H. Berzins 1982.

1977 August 20, **Samba Pa Ti**, Dow Crag, A. Hyslop, R. Graham.

1977 September 4, **Prana**, Black Crag, P. Gommersal.

1980 June 26, **Fear and Fascination**, Dove Crag, R. Graham, B. Birkett (shar).